TOWARDS THE HUMAN

TOWARDS THE HUMAN

Selected Essays

by

IAIN CRICHTON SMITH

With an Introduction by
DERICK THOMSON

LINES REVIEW EDITIONS

MACDONALD PUBLISHERS
EDINBURGH

© Iain Crichton Smith 1986

ISBN 0 86334 059 8

Published in 1986 by
Macdonald Publishers
Loanhead, Midlothian EH20 9SY

The publisher acknowledges the financial assistance of the Scottish Arts Council in the publication of this volume

Printed in Scotland by
Macdonald Printers (Edinburgh) Limited
Edgefield Road, Loanhead, Midlothian EH20 9SY

Contents

Introductory Note by Derick Thomson	7
PART ONE	
Real People in a Real Place	13
PART TWO: THE POET'S WORLD	
Between Sea and Moor	73
A Poet in Scotland	84
Poetic Energy, Language and Nationhood	87
PART THREE: THE GAELIC POET	
Modern Gaelic Poetry	97
George Campbell Hay: Language at Large	108
The Modest Doctor: The Poetry of Donald MacAulay	116
Gaelic Master: Sorley MacLean	123
Duncan Ban MacIntyre	132
The Poetry of Derick Thomson	136
A Note on Gaelic Criticism	144
PART FOUR: SCOTTISH POETRY	
The Feeling Intelligence	149
Sea Talk by George Bruce	154
Towards the Human: The Poetry of Stewart Conn	159
The Power of Craftsmanship: The Poetry of Robert Garioch	167
Hugh MacDiarmid: *A Drunk Man Looks at the Thistle*	171
The Golden Lyric: An Essay on the Poetry of Hugh MacDiarmid	176
The Complete Poems of Hugh MacDiarmid	192
MacDiarmid and Ideas, with special reference to "On a Raised Beach"	194
SELECT BIBLIOGRAPHY	200

Acknowledgements

The author and publisher are grateful to the following for permission to republish the following essays: Robert Hale Ltd, "Between Sea and Moor"; *Poetry Dimension Annual*, "A Poet in Scotland"; *The Scottish Review*, "Poetic Energy, Language and Nationhood", "George Campbell Hay: Language at Large", "Gaelic Master: Sorley MacLean", "The Poetry of Derick Thomson"; *Gairm*, "The Modest Doctor: The Poetry of Donald Macaulay"; *The Scotsman*, "Duncan Ban MacIntyre; *New Edinburgh Review*, "Towards the Human: The Poetry of Stewart Conn"; *Studies in Scottish Literature*, "Hugh MacDiarmid: *A Drunk Man Looks at the Thistle*"; Akros Publications, "The Golden Lyric: An Essay on the Poetry of Hugh MacDiarmid"; *The Glasgow Herald*, "The Complete Poems of Hugh MacDiarmid".

The following essays are previously unpublished and appear for the first time in this volume: "Real People in a Real Place", "A Note on Gaelic Criticism", "The Feeling Intelligence", "*Sea Talk* by George Bruce", "The Power of Craftsmanship: The Poetry of Robert Garioch", "MacDiarmid and Ideas, with special reference to 'On a Raised Beach'."

Introductory Note

The writer in a small country has to face problems and choices that are unfamiliar to writers in a larger one, and there are further complications when the language used is a minority one, or worse, one which appears to be approaching extinction at some finite point in time. The choices may also be challenges, so that we are not talking necessarily about a gloomy situation, but rather a different one.

One thing that is reasonably certain is that if there is no sense of challenge there will be little of interest in the writing that results. The status quo is not good enough in these circumstances. And any sort of retreat behind a perimeter, or into a reservation mentality, has acute dangers for the writer. It is almost certainly better, and healthier, to look outwards, and bring fresh literary experience to bear on the native tradition.

All this is not to say that the writer should turn his back on the society, or experience, that is native to him. If he does he may succeed in some specialist sense, but is hardly likely to write work that is deeply significant. This may be especially true of the poet, who draws on subconscious resources for an important part of his work.

In the Gaelic case it is important that the writer should feel as free to write about, say, drug traffic or apartheid or space travel, as anyone else who has information and opinions on these matters. Equally it is important for the health of the language that people should write about new or unfamiliar topics. And the healths of language and literature are deeply intertwined. Translation from foreign literatures is another important medium of transfusion, and it is for these reasons that the Gaelic magazine *Gairm*, for example, has over the last three decades and more, encouraged a wider subject range as well as translation. Iain Crichton Smith, like George Campbell Hay before him and Christopher Whyte more recently, has done valuable translating work, and has always been ready to experiment with subject and language.

The same arguments would hold for writing in Scots, with Garioch a fine example of their value. But there has to be a change of focus to enable us to see the parallel in the case of Scottish writing in English, though the value of the transfusions may be equally crucial.

To some extent what I have been saying does not fully apply to Iain Crichton Smith. He has written more in English than in Gaelic, and could choose to belong to an English tradition of writing more than a Gaelic one. He still has the problems of Scottish location and Gaelic primary experience to resolve. And since he continues to write in Gaelic, he has to make his specific decisions there also.

The present collection of essays shows that all these problems are close to him, and since they are, an understanding of how he sees them, and reacts to them, is bound to throw light on his other writing. His uneasy struggle with the two worlds of Gaelic and English comes alive repeatedly. Occasionally it is over-dramatised, it seems to me, and certainly there is much that is "read back," from a later standpoint, into the early experience of these two worlds. The first long essay, "Real people in a real place," once it gets past the generalisations of the opening pages (especially the references to tourist assessments of the islands), and becomes more specific, is a true confrontation with the central dilemma of Gaelic and island life. It would be unreal to expect a historian's or sociologist's summing-up here. It is better to have the artist's individual response, not complete or balanced, even myopic at times, but with an individual focus which gives it its own validity.

Having been brought up in the same village as Iain, and having gone to the same schools, and Aberdeen University, I find myself with a rather different set of reactions, and would find room for many literary symbols besides his Penguin New Writing one. But fundamentally I agree with what he says about community in this essay, and regard that as the core of it.

There and elsewhere throughout the collection he comes back obsessively to poetry, always pondering the ultimate nature of poetry, isolating as best he can what belongs to that nature. There is an obvious degree of repetition as where he gathers together essays published at different times on Gaelic poetry, and essays on individual poets. We can see, sometimes, how his critical responses have changed with the years, becoming less dogmatic and, I think, less confident (in a good sense). We could have done with a longer and more developed "Note on Gaelic criticism," where he says, for example, that there is no point in comparing Duncan Ban MacIntyre with Wordsworth, and refers to "the catalogues of Gaelic adjectives such as we get in Duncan Ban MacIntyre and in Alexander MacDonald" as "a menace to the development of good poetry, though we find them being used as late as Sorley MacLean. . . ." Perhaps these matters need more detailed argument, and contrary cases might be made in both instances. But these are useful examples of how some of his remarks can be used as starting points for further discussion.

The essays on Scottish poets who have written in Scots and English are full of individual interest. The essay on George Bruce's poetry is based on the harsh idea "It is in fact the poetry of a region that does not believe in poetry," and it gnaws at this concept so persistently that one begins uncomfortably to believe in it. The essay on Garioch similarly teases out the quiddity of that poet's work. And in the essays on Hugh MacDiarmid we see him using the work as a series of touchstones to guide him, steadily one often feels, towards the ultimate core of poetry. In "The Feeling Intelligence," we find him suggesting that this is a poetic road too often blocked for the Scottish writer. He concludes the essay in this way: "For Scotland's poet there awaits logic, scholarship, metaphysics, but there also awaits, if he has the patience of the feeling intelligence, the living quick of life itself. Perhaps he should choose the latter more in future, if his tangled languages, his education, his claustrophobia, will allow him."

That quotation brings us very close to the nerve centre of this collection of essays, and it touches on many of the interests that are pursued, in less concentrated form, in others of the essays. It may also be the ideal towards which the author's own poetry has been gradually moving.

The mixture of autobiography, criticism, reflection on society, and literary theory, against a reflected background of wide reading in poetry in a number of different traditions, is a stimulating one which must make us think again about the practice, and purpose, and the nature of writing, and especially writing poetry, in Scotland, while the collection throws light continually on the author's own creative work.

DERICK S. THOMSON

Part One

Real People in a Real Place

Real People in a Real Place

... The difficulty is not alone a want of native moulds; it is rather the want of a foundation upon which to establish them. Everywhere in the mentality of the Irish people are flux and uncertainty. Our national consciousness may be described, in a native phrase, as a quaking sod. It gives no footing. It is not English, nor Irish, nor Anglo-Irish; as will be understood if one thinks a while on the thwarting it undergoes in each individual child of the race as he grows into manhood. Though not quite true, let us take it that the Irish-born child is as Irish in his instincts, in his emotions, as the English child is English: the period of education comes on: all that the English child learns buttresses, while it refines, his emotional nature. Practically all the literature he reads focuses for him the mind of his own people; so also does the instruction he hears. At a later stage if he comes to read a foreign language he seizes what he reads in it with an English mind. He has something of his own by which to estimate its value for him.

How different with the Irish child! No sooner does he begin to use his intellect than what he learns begins to undermine, to weaken, and to harass his emotional nature. For practically all that he reads is English—what he reads in Irish is not yet worth taking account of. It does not therefore focus the mind of his own people, teaching him the better to look about him, to understand both himself and his surroundings. It focuses instead the life of another people. Instead of sharpening his gaze upon his own neighbourhood, his reading distracts it, for he cannot find in these surroundings what his reading has taught him is the matter worth coming upon. His surroundings begin to seem unvital. His education, instead of buttressing and refining his emotional nature, teaches him rather to despise it, inasmuch as it teaches him not to see the surroundings out of which he is sprung, as they are in themselves, but as compared with alien surroundings: his education provides him with an alien medium through which he is henceforth to look at his native land! At the least his education sets up a dispute between his intellect and his emotions. Nothing happens in the neighbourhood of an English boy's home—the fair, the hurling match, the land grabbing, the *priesting* the mission, the Mass—he never comes on in literature, that is, in such literature as he is told to respect and learn. Evidently what happens in his own fields is not stuff for the Muses!

—Daniel Corkery: *Synge and Anglo-Irish Literature* (1931)

To grow up on an island is to grow up in a special world. Many of the books that I have read on the Hebrides, however, make this world appear Edenic and unreal: others suggest that the islander is a child who appears lost in the "real world," and even invent for him a language that was never spoken by anyone. It is easy to assign the islander to this misty, rather beautiful world, and leave him there if one first of all succeeds in making that world unreal, and its inhabitants unreal, off the edge of things, a noble savage with his stories and his unmaterialistic concerns. After all, is he not a Celt and are the Celts not meant to be rather vague, impractical, poetical, not at all like "us," who succeed in both admiring and patronising the natives, simultaneously accepting that it would be nice to be poetic (and after all the islanders are nice) and also believing that such niceness is not after all suitable to the world in which we live.

These books do not take the islander seriously as a real person in a real place: he is the being but not the person that we meet on holiday when we are released from the cares of the admittedly imperfect but thoroughly twentieth-century world from which we come. Thus the islander is seen as the pawky ferryman whom one meets at the entrance to the enchanted land of summer, when the country to which he belongs is beautiful and slightly hazy, a place for a holiday. After this interlude, the real world with its constant grind and envy and ambition is waiting for us, but it is nice to think that the islanders exist behind and beyond it, as a haven beyond the edge of the sharp rocks which await us. The islander is not a menace to us, he is the tame feed for our happy comedy, he makes no demands. Why should he? Does he not have after all a beautiful place in which to stay, that blue morning of the world in which he doesn't have to work too hard, in which he actually welcomes the slightly silly but, of course, really superior tourist.

The visitor does not admit that he himself is slightly silly, that is only part of the game. If he were to think that, in that environment, then the islander would be a threat to him (which he is not), he would become a real person (which he is not). To admit that he is a real person would immediately place him in the centre of the world from which the tourist has come, with all the difficulties and treacheries that such a world contains.

To see him as an individual would surround him with the real pathos of the real person, with the envies which surround the tourist himself. No, the islander must not have materialistic concerns, or if he has they must be transformed into comedy, as in the film *Whisky Galore*. The real desire for that which he has not got, which everyone feels, must be dissipated in clouds of whisky: the islanders must become little children who have no lust for possessions as corrupt as that of the mainlanders, but are simply enacting a play for the benefit of the stranger. And this can be best done by inventing a language for him which will itself be as ludicrous as the language given to the Red Indians in Westerns. Such a language (with its "whateffers" and similar infusions) was never spoken by an islander, but that does not matter. It is a language which he would speak if he knew how. At any rate it is a method of differentiating him from those who have a real language and can speak it. It would after all be too ridiculous to have to learn Gaelic, the real language of the islander, as English is to the tourist. The very fact that the islander needs to speak English but can't is in itself a source of patronage. It does not seem to occur to the tourist that the islander can speak perfect English, as far as perfection of English can be said to exist. The tourists do not hear this grammatical English, so conditioned are they to expect a broken one.

In this way the islander is labelled, surrounded by mythology, so that the meanest tourist can feel himself superior to the brightest islander. After all, if the islander were bright, in the sense that brightness is considered important, how could he possibly stay in the islands? To be a native must surely mean that he could not have made it elsewhere. Nor does the tourist see how ridiculous it is to think that he has any superiority to the natives, many of whom have travelled the world, having been forced to do so. No, the islander must be considered as having always lived in this enchanted unreal world, with its mountains and its lochs and its sunsets. To admit that he has chosen to live here, after living in other places, would immediately smash the image, it would mean that he has chosen not to live, for instance, in the place the tourists have come from and that he refuses to admit that theirs is the real world. And how could they then patronise him? How could one consider him the unmaterialistic child who has succeeded in remaining where he is, free of ambitions and corrupt emotions by simply being who he is, the eternally innocent.

And, of course, the tourist is wrong, for the islander, just like anybody else, is concerned with ambition and all the other emotions that corrupt the inhabitants of the world. He too desires possessions, he too wishes to do well for himself, for if that were not the case he would not be human. Nor does it occur to the tourist (in the same way as it does not occur to the white Australian who despises the aborigine) that he himself would find it more difficult to survive in the conditions in which the islander has to live than he would in his own place. For it cannot be emphasised too often that the tourist meets the islander in the summer when the land is more enchanted than it would normally appear, and it is with the islands in the summer that many travel books deal. For the summer is the period when we relax from the hard grind of the rest of the year, when returning energy makes us see the world in a new light, as if it really is not at all as bad as we had thought it was, as if it is truly a gift. Then the tourist sheds his worries as he travels into the centre of this world, he meets with what he hopes to meet, the one who is more innocent than himself, who seems to live in an eternal summer, who is forever at play.

Nor does he look behind the face of the man whom he meets, nor does he see the irony which is patent to the islander. For the islander regards the tourist as one who lives on the surface of what he sees, and the tourist, on the other hand, while seeming to admit this, at the same time knows, really knows, that his world is more gritty, more real, and therefore he can afford to make fun of himself, as if he were in a wonderland. But this is only a pretence, and a form of superiority, for if he were to admit for one moment that the islander could seriously make fun of him, what would become of this lovable wonderland? It is because he cannot conceive that the islander can really make fun of him that he can afford to appear so vulnerable. After all, laughter does not belong to the real world.

He would also refuse to admit that the world of the islander can change. It remains for him a perpetually unchanging world since he does not see beyond the mask that he has himself constructed. He would be staggered to realise how much the world of the islander has changed in its inner workings. To confess that this is so can only be predicated on the assumption that it is a real world, just like the one from which he has come. And if he does admit that it has changed, if he once sees a glimpse of the other world beyond this happily dancing one, then he becomes angry. It is as if this enchanted world has betrayed him, as if this world which in any case was never as he had thought it was, showed a face which is not all that different from the world which he left. This explains why the world of the islander is often attacked by those who once loved it, in a way that they would never attack the outside world from which they have come. Such people are like those who have left behind them the enchantments of Communism which was never in any case what they had thought it was.

The tourist, however, does not realise that he is in a similar position to the islander who has left the island, usually for economic reasons, in his youth. The islander who is living in the city is like the tourist in that he does not want to acknowledge change either, he wants the islands to belong to the world which he too has created, one of happy boyhood, perpetual summers, nice, kind people, lack of ambition and adult emotions. He too wishes to return to a place where doors were never locked, where crime was unimaginable, where real sorrow was not to be found, from which death had been banished. He too returns in summer, and when he sees television sets in the houses, regrets their presence as if the islanders had somehow let him down. Why, the islands are just like the city. How could the islanders have betrayed him so profoundly, so cheated him of his dream?

Thus the tourist and the exiled islander belong to a similar species, each deceiving himself, though the reasons are not exactly the same. For the islander, exile leads to bad poetry; for the tourist, who has no experience of real exile, it leads to a dream without substance. But the exile has in fact lived in the islands and his self-deception is the greater. He may even be happy in the city though he may try to convince himself that this cannot be true, for if it were true what would happen to those sunny boyhood days, that stainless summer? He surely cannot be happy in the city, for that would be a denial of the logic of nostalgia. But because he is a human being there is no reason why he should be happy in the city: thus he too does a disservice to the islander by making him unreal. And his poetry also does a disservice by referring to an eternal perfection of childhood, for the poetry of exile is nearly always bad. He exists in what Sartre might call "bad faith." Yet why should he? There is no reason why as a particular person he shouldn't feel happy in the city: there is no law which states otherwise. Yet he feels guilty about it, as if he has committed some treason against his race.

It is true that when he first went to the city he might have felt it menacing and inhuman, and at such moments he might withdraw into the world of childhood which might by contrast appear innocent and precious. But as he conquered the city, as he became self-confident within it, why should he still feel guilty? Why should he feel as if he had committed the greatest of all sins, the betrayal of his own country, the country of illusion which in self-defence he created and which he can now throw away. In remaining inside his guilt and his illusion he equally does a disservice to those who stay in the islands and who wish to do so, and for whom the islands is their reality.

Another kind of disservice is to think that the islander really wants to leave his island. It is only stubbornness and tradition which make him stay, irritating governments, making subsidies essential. Such a view arises from the fact that governments see only what they want to see, they do not understand that they are dealing with real people and that, like all real people, they wish to inhabit their own homes. For the bureaucrat, the tourist, the exile, the islander is not a real person, and therefore it is not easy to see him at all. He is invisible in the misty place he inhabits.

Why should the islander not be allowed to see his home as a home, as the place he wants to be in? There is no doubt that for most of us home is the place where there are resonances which never again are to be found elsewhere, though that is not to say that these resonances belong to a dream. Home is the place where we feel right, wherever that home may be. For the exile it may be the city, though he refuses to believe it, for the islander it is the island where he lives. There is too much guilt associated with the islands, and this guilt is the more exaggerated the more one thinks of them as an unreal place. The islands were never an Eden from which we were thrust by the sword of economics: it may have been a home but it was never an Eden. Nor is this to say that we don't blame the insensitivity of bureaucrats and others but rather to say that though it was made difficult for us to live at home, that home was never in itself a paradise, any more than the desert was for the aborigine.

To grow up on an island is a special experience, but it is not an ideal experience. It is one of many possible experiences, it is a real experience; it is chosen by those who choose, and for those who do not choose it is the same as any other home, with certain difficulties.

When one reads poems like the "Canadian Boat Song," one sees that the exile has accepted the judgment of the imperialist who has dislodged him. Who, he asks, will fight for him in the future, asking the wrong question, for it was the interior colonisation of the islander that made him proud of being a soldier. There is nothing here but dream after dream, each entwined, like a Chinese box, within the next. And all those exiles who come home from Canada in "Scottish Week" or whatever, what are they coming home to? To a theatre that has been carefully arranged and plotted to receive them, to a dream that has been carefully scripted. It is possible that those Canadians and Americans have come to the midpoint of their lives only to find that they are alone, as all of us are alone, and that what they spent their lives seeking no longer has any savour for them. And so they return to their roots only to be exploited by those who clear-sightedly exploit the world of the islander. Those who exploit them are not the islanders, for the islanders see them in their fancy kilts as comic: and yet they perhaps see too the human pathos that has made them what they are. The islander does not exploit that impossible dream which they follow.

When the islander's own brother or sister comes home from

America or Canada he welcomes them, but he does not welcome them into a dream. He knows that they left because they *had* to leave or because they wished to avoid facing up to the responsibilities of the island world. He is not easily deceived. He knows that much has had to be abandoned to earn the success such exiles have earned, and he does not gloat if they return as failures. For the failures are those who have had human aspirations also, and perhaps set off into another dream, that of Australia or Canada. When he sees them coming home he sees only the failure of another dream, and is tender with those who, while failures, refuse to admit that they are so. For home is for everyone who wishes it to be their home. But he sees also through the hypocrisy of the successful who think that they can have both worlds, the ruthless ambition of the one, and the unreal, stainless happiness of the other.

It is the dismissal of the islander as if he were not intelligent, as if he did not judge as other people judge, that is the most irritating thing of all, and the cause of the central error. The islander reacts to human situations as everyone else does. It is true that like everyone else he wishes his brother to be successful, but he does not think that success is everything, nor is he easily conned by the photographs of prosperity which are sent home so regularly, sometimes as Christmas cards. There are relative degrees of success after all, and success at the expense of those who stay behind may not be highly regarded. Success is always at the expense of someone, and it is not the case that the islander's reaction is always: "Look, he has proved in the outside world that all islanders can be successful if they choose." There are other criteria of success: it was not the richest individual that the islanders always looked up to, rather they looked up to the schoolmaster and the minister, whose success is not to be measured in money. Nevertheless change is always possible, for the islander, no more than other people, remains fixed, and it may be that money, naked money, will come to be considered important. To live is to change and the islander lives in the real world which is the real world of all of us, and the arts of that world will exert an influence on him, as perhaps he himself exerts an influence on others.

It is not that the returning exile passes judgment on the islander who has remained behind: the islander too exerts his judgment on the exile as he does on the tourist. Though he may not speak much, that does not mean that he does not think, and it is perhaps a certain kind of vulgarity that disgusts him most, like the aristocrat who talks too loudly as if the whole world were his parlour, and his interests the central ones. The Highlander has a concept of *cliù*, which roughly means "reputation," and such a concept implies that a man who has it may be considered useful to the community, not glorified, but respected. The blatant colours of the returning exile, however preposterous, are too bright for him: he wishes to be known as one who belongs to a community and who does service to that community.

To be an islander is to inhabit real space on a real earth. He too has to make choices in the real world where he is: he too has an attitude to that place. He has his proverbs, his philosophies, the cemeteries and cradles of his hopes: his tasks and his loves: his language. Behind the judgment made on him by the bureaucrat is the idea that his world is in some way irrelevant, without challenge, an evasion: as if men at all times were always making decisions when in fact they are making similar decisions, once the local variations have been accounted for. If to live on the islands is to be different, is to die on the islands also different? Is it a different thing to count one's housekeeping money on the islands, or is that too sordid? In fact the islander has to make the hardest choice of all, since, for instance, in education he has to ask himself, "Should my daughter take French at the expense of Gaelic?" For if there is no Gaelic left, will not the islander live in a disappearing landscape, as an Englishman would if his language were slowly to die?

It is true that more than most the islander is caught in a net of contradictions, imposed on him by history, and that to live from the centre of what he is, is far harder than for those who have been luckier with their geography and their history.

The problem of language is obviously of the first importance. If the islander were to speak English and still inhabit the island which he does in fact inhabit, what would he be then but an unreal person in an unreal place? If he were to wake one morning and look around him and see "hill" and not "*cnoc*," would he not be an expatriate of his own land? What if an Englishman were to waken one morning and see that "tree" had been transformed to "*arbre*"? He would have the psychology of the exile who on landing in Nova Scotia were to see a Red Indian and hear his strange language which he would be unable to understand. For we are born inside a language and see everything from within its parameters: it is not we who make language, it is language that makes us.

Thus for me to go home to my island and talk to my Gaelic-speaking brother in English would be to establish a distance between us that would not just be linguistic but social. Gaelic is the language of the islands, and not the broken English of the island Red Indian as heard, for instance, in the books of Lilian Beckwith. And for Gaelic to die would be for the islands to die a more profound death than economics could bring. The imperialism of language is the most destructive of all and indeed we can see this when we admit that a word like *cliù* in

Gaelic is really untranslatable, implying as it does a community, and not the reputation of, say, a film star or pop star.

To feel free as far as man can, and to begin from that freedom, is what we all wish. For an Englishman, secure in his own world, to study French literature does not seem to be a form of treachery: and yet because of the guilt that his conditions impose on him, on the bright as well as the not so bright, for the islander to be influenced by T. S. Eliot or William Carlos Williams instead of by Duncan Ban MacIntyre is almost to be a traitor. To write in English becomes a form of treachery and this is so because Gaelic does not have the strength to allow explorations into language beyond itself. If Gaelic had that strength then for someone from within to write in another language would appear the most sublime form of self-confidence; to introduce new ideas, new concepts, would be a service which would be analogous to the introduction into English of foreign words, fresh philosophies. Thus the creative writer is constrained by the weakness of his own language, and his adventurousness becomes treachery. He too is forced to choose in a real place and his choices reverberate down his life story.

A broken land broken by history and the actions of men makes all choices into snakes that have multiple intricate windings. They rear up out of that supposedly naïve greenery and their beauty is their treachery. It is not true that the writer who comes from such a place belongs to any misty twilight. The best Gaelic poetry has always been the clearest and the sunniest and the most humanly penetrating. The choices for the gifted islander are more poignant and frequent than they would be in a more settled land, for each choice appears to involve allegiance or disloyalty.

The fact of the islands stronger than any other is that of exile: it is that which casts its guilt continually backwards like the rays of a setting sun. The islander has never had the chance of staying where he is: history has condemned him to departure, and afterwards to the choice of whether or not to return. Thus the home becomes for him more important than it does for others and the temptation to idealise it immense and almost forgivable. When the home is shifting continually then one feels compelled to name it, and sometimes to do so falsely. The fact of the exile leads to the lie which is intended to comfort and to fix the home. Thus there is talk of the warmth and the honesty and the love: thus we find a line like:

> There is no ceilidh on the prairie.

For the ceilidh represented the community that joined together in entertainment created from within itself. Stories would be told, songs would be sung. As Derick Thomson has pointed out in an interesting poem concerned with the destructiveness of a certain kind of doctrine, when the fire was moved from the centre of the floor then the magic ring was broken.

THE SCARECROW

That night
the scarecrow came into the ceilidh-house:
a tall, thin black-haired man
wearing black clothes.
He sat on the bench
and the cards fell from our hands.
One man
was telling a folktale about Conall Gulban
and the words froze on his lips.
A woman was sitting on a stool,
singing songs, and he took the goodness out of the music.
But he did not leave us empty-handed:
he gave us a new song,
and tales from the Middle East,
and fragments of the philosophy of Geneva,
and he swept the fire from the centre of the floor
and set a searing bonfire in our breasts.

(trans. Derick Thomson)

In this poem Thomson is making a profound statement using fire imagery to describe the destruction of a community. The fire became internalised as hell, which was once the fire, common and warm and storied, which nourished the island house. Exile, too, took the fire from the middle of the floor and put it searing in the breasts of the exiles.

To be an exile is to be a double man, living in a new world while still enchanted by the fantasies of the old. In Nova Scotia the new exiles gave the names of their old homes to a new land: thus Campbeltown, Loch Lomond, and so on: it was as if the islander wished to waken in the morning surrounded by the village from which he had sailed, as a child by well-loved dolls in a new house. But the gauntness of the day showed that the names were after all not spells but crutches. In the beginning they were the nomenclatures of men's sanities, anchors, but later they were transformed and became part of the country to which they now belonged, for new skin had grown over the old wound.

Whenever one visits Canada or Australia one feels that pathos of the exile, the failure and the success. The exile sings Gaelic songs (sometimes knows more verses than the native does) and his dream is unbroken. But it is always anachronistic, the home has left him behind, and this because it belongs to a real land in a real place. As he moves towards it, it recedes forever as the water did from Tantalus.

Thus the songs sung at modern ceilidhs have nothing at all to do with those sung at the old ceilidhs. The new ceilidh has now become a concert, with "stars" in kilts twinkling from platforms in great halls in Glasgow or Edinburgh. The songs have become nostalgic exercises, a method of freezing time, of stopping the real traffic of Sauchiehall Street, a magic evocation of a lost island in the middle of the city. The traditional ceilidh which was held in the village ceilidh house was a celebration of the happenings of the village, it was alive, it was a diary and a repeated record. The ceilidh as it is now practised is a treacherous weakening of the present, a memorial, a tombstone on what has once been, pipes playing in a graveyard. It was not of such ceilidhs that the poet wrote, "There is no ceilidh on the prairie." He was thinking of the traditional ceilidh, the guarantee of a society. And since the word *céilidh* could also mean a visit, he meant that in that vastness there was no traditional visiting. To contrast the ceilidh with the prairie was to contrast the small with the gigantic, the human with the inhuman. It was to contrast a community with a void.

For when I was growing up on the island of Lewis people would go into houses without knocking, doors were never locked. This is not nostalgia but truth. I was in other people's houses as often as I was in my own. Houses were not locked since stealing was an inconceivable crime. Indeed crime was itself inconceivable, for to commit a crime was forever to lose one's *cliù*, one's reputation, one's status in the community, and that would last, because of the communal memory to the end of time. The judgment was indeed to the fourth generation and beyond. There was a policeman but there was no need for one. Why should there be when the community itself passed judgment? A judgment what was more rigorous than any that the law could impose. I know in fact of no crime (punishable by law) that was committed by the community all the time that I was growing up there.

It is this sense of a community that one thinks of most when one compares the island with the city. It was because of the community that the fact of exile became so desolating and frightening. For to become an exile is to become an individual on one's own in a world in which there is no community. It is not leaving the island or the village that is the terrible thing, it is leaving the community. There are, of course, two sides to the community, the positive and the negative. The positive is the sense of warmth, settledness, that it gives, the feeling that one has a place, a name, that one will not be consigned to the chilly air of pure individuality. It is the sense that what one belongs to is a sustaining force, that one is held up in its buoyancy as a swimmer in water. When one is in harmony with the community then one's identity is reflected back from the others by a plain mirror and not by the exaggerating or attenuating mirrors that one sees in fairs. To be in the community is to be in a home of which one's real home is a microcosm: thus it is that when one goes out into the wide world one comes back to receive the admiration of the community, if one does well.

During the war when I was growing up any boys who were home on leave were expected to visit all the houses in the community: and when one goes home to the island one would be forever despised if one stayed in a town hotel rather than in one of the village houses. To return home is not simply to return home, it is to return to a community, for one's gains or losses to be assessed. The community is the ultimate critic, not easily taken in, with its own system of checks and balances. To be part of the community is in a sense to belong to everyone, to be open, vulnerable, to be willing to abide by its judgment.

In the old days, too, much of the work was communal. Thus the carrying home of the peats was a communal activity. One helped others and was in turn helped by them. The day of the carrying home of the peats was a meeting of the community in an exchange of stories, badinage, gossip. One's place in the community was precisely known and its judgment in general was a practical one. The events of the community were immortalised by the local bard, humorously and pungently. The community was as delicate as a spider's web: if you pulled one part the rest would tremble. It was a feat of almost instinctive engineering.

It is far more difficult to live in a community than to live in a city, for in a community one must have an awareness of the parameters beyond which one cannot go. For the islander to enter the city was to enter a totally new kind of world which in many cases caused "culture shock," not so much because of the demands that the city made, but because of its impersonality, because one was no longer sustained by communal force.

One of my clearest memories is at the age of seventeen arriving at Aberdeen Railway Station and finding sitting there a beggar in black glasses with a cap in front of him on the pavement and in it a few pennies. Such a sight would have been unheard of in an island community. The beggar's blatant economic demand and his overt helplessness, this individual throwing himself on the mercy of chance, would have been a contradiction of everything that the community represented. The shame of dropping out of the community to become pure individuality in a void would not be a concept that a community could sustain.

The city would have been the most terrifying place of all to a person brought up in a community and whose name was known to everybody. Its events would appear inexplicable accidents, its individual pains would demand a return to those warm characteristics of the community which would appear as almost unbearable nostalgia. For if there was ambition in the community it was thought that ambition should be in its service: thus the minister and the teacher were the archetypal figures rather than the rich, since their work was in the service of the community. Nor was it I think clear to the community, with its clarity which one later achieves, that the teacher was in fact educating the children out of the community.

A poem like the following shows quite clearly what the results of nostalgia would be when the islander confronted the city. It is called "When I was Young" and was written by the nineteenth-century Skye poetess Mary Macpherson:

> I wakened early, with little sadness,
> on a morning in May in Òs;
> with cattle lowing as they gathered,
> with the sun rising on Leac an Stòir;
> Its rays were shining on the mountains,
> covering over in haste night's gloom;
> the lively lark sang her song above me,
> reminding me of when I was young.
>
> . . . . . .
>
> It brought to mind many things I did then,
> though some eluded me for all my days,
> going in winter to waulkings, weddings,
> no light from lantern but a burning peat;
> there were lively youngsters, and song and dancing,
> but that is gone and the glen is sad;
> Andrew's ruins overgrown with nettles
> reminded me of when I was young.
>
> When I walked by each glen and hillock
> where I once was carefree, herding cows,
> with happy youths who have now been banished,
> the native stock without pride or guile,
> the fields and plains were under heath and rushes
> where I often cut wisps and sheaves of corn;
> could I but see folk and houses there now
> my heart were light as when I was young.
>
> <div align="right">(<i>trans.</i> Derick Thomson)</div>

The contradictions in island life become dizzying and prolific precisely because we are dealing with a community which has been broken by history. Such historical accident does not argue against the idea of community, though it is quite possible that in the same way as trade unions arose to protect the indigent, communities are strongest when the level of economic power is not high.

What we are concerned with are the human gifts that the community endows, and the principal one is the sense of security that it gives, that no city can give, unless one joins artificial substitutes such as clubs of various kinds. The strength of the island community is that one is born into it. When I was growing up there was no work done on the day of a funeral, for death was respected. To withdraw from the community was the greatest sin that one could commit. At all costs the balance must be maintained, the miraculous and precarious balance. To be forced to live in a community and not be part of it would be a sort of refined hell. Thus it is that I have always believed there is a point even in our schools when they can be a community, and when that point is transcended there is an increase in crime among those who are not named, are not recognised.

As we are talking about a real people in a real place, we have to admit that the community also has its negative side, that is to say it is nearly always conservative and hostile to change. There is a dislike of the person who individualises himself too much, who tries to succeed for his own purposes.

When I left the village community in order to attend the secondary school in Stornoway I felt as if I was abandoning the community. There was a subtle alteration to me in the attitude of my contemporaries who were not taking the road of education but would work on the land or on the fishing boats. Even now when I meet members of the community who have stayed at home there is a slight constraint in our relationship, there is a human distance. I have made the choice, I have forsaken the community in order to individualise myself.

Even when I was quite young I felt this problem in a minor, but for me important, decision. When I used to play football I was asked both to play for the town school and the village school. I chose to play for the village because in a deep way I sensed that my allegiance was to it.

As well as this I was confronted by a language dilemma, for when I was in the town during the day I spoke English all the time, whereas when I came home to the village every evening I spoke Gaelic. All these things seem in retrospect to have been a series of consequences which flowed from an original decision, if one takes a decision at such an early age. I became schizophrenic for, as I have already said, to have spoken English in the village would have been not a linguistic gesture but a social one. I look back with a pitying contempt at the person I was and remember that when I was asked to write an obituary for a boy who had died in the village I quoted from Paul Valery. I had myself beeen taken in by the propaganda which made foreign writing more serious, more interesting, more advanced.

And one of the reasons for this was, there were no children's books in Gaelic which I might have read even if, in my arrogance, I had wanted to do so. Though I was brought up on an island where Gaelic was the dominant language, my reading was much the same as if I had been educated at Eton, rather than at Bayble Public School, that is to say, Penguin New Writing, among whose contributors were, of course, Auden, Spender and MacNeice.

I have already said that the community tends to be conservative by nature. It can also be claustrophobic, in the same way as a family can be claustrophobic, for one is known as the person one is, forever. One's parents are known, one's grandparents are known, one is in an assigned position. When I left the community to go to Aberdeen University, I felt paradoxically free since I could walk down Union Street without anyone knowing who I was. Invisibility became important to me, it was as if I had cast off chains, as the ship does when it leaves harbour. To leave the community was to emerge into one's individuality, into a future which seemed free and unjudged, though of course it was not. On the island I had felt religion as a restricting force, but the fact that I have wrestled so much with a particular kind of religion in my poetry suggests that I do not have the ease to discuss it freely. Religion had been internalised in my personality whether I like it or not and its dilemmas will always be with me.

The contemporary writer who seems to me to have analysed the concept of community most clearly and most perceptively is Donald MacAulay, the modern Gaelic poet. Like Derick Thomson, he has analysed the influence of Calvinism, as in the poem, "Self Righteousness":

> They ask of me only
> to weep repentance for a sin
> that does not concern me
> and I shall get in return an alien
> freedom I don't understand:
> to be drubbed in one thin,
> wounding water after another
> of their philosophy—
> and confidently they would
> hang
> their washing in the heavens.
>
> (*trans.* Donald MacAulay)

The poem is, I think, self-explanatory, comparing as it does the new repentant person to freshly washed clothes. More subtle is "Landmark," which contains most fully the windings and intricacies of what an island home means:

> There goes the island out of sight
> as the boat sails on,
> as seen by many a bard
> through sorrow and beer
> and by others, tongue under tooth,
> and tears blinding—
> and ill-defined shadow and windows fading.
>
> But the matter is not so simple
> to the one who's a yearly pilgrim:
> out of returning, sorrow rises
> from a region the world has derided.
>
> And, that is not my island:
> it submerged long ago
> the greater part of it
> in neglect and tyranny—
> and the part that submerged in me of it,
> sun-bower and iceberg,
> sails the ocean I travel,
> a primary landmark
> dangerous, essential, demanding.
>
> (trans. Donald MacAulay)

As one listens to the songs in the saloon of the departing ship, one knows that they are composed of nostalgia but also emerge from alcohol. In the first few lines, the poet is concerned with the departing exile, but later he talks of the "yearly pilgrim"—as if the annual return to the island were a religious rite—and it is the one who returns who can compare the world of the island with the so-called real world. The sorrow rises out of the placing beside each other of this picture and that: the exile sees the island in the derisive light cast by the world from which he has briefly come. Nor is the island that he sees on his return the same one as he has left—for when he left he had nothing to compare the island to: now he sees it not with the earlier innocence and idealism but as a mockery of what it once was.

Nevertheless that earlier island, that first innocence untested by experience, has been internalised in his consciousness: it is the "primary landmark, dangerous, essential, demanding." Some of these dangers and demands have already been commented upon. The island is compared to an iceberg, for an iceberg has more of its mass below the surface than above it. It changes continually in the mind, now larger now smaller, set against the world which lies outside it and yet essentially mobile, lonely, ghostly. The demands of the island are incessant for to leave it is to have convicted oneself of a crime. It is the court of law, the cold iceberg which judges one eternally.

More closely related to the community as such is the poem "A Delicate Balance," which might very well be chosen as an epigraph for the community. This poem is MacAulay's clear-eyed, humane examination of the problem of the community, its ultimate enigma.

> You suffered ignominy
> and shame,
> a butt for slight and mockery—
> if you spoke a word
> they dived on it
> like gannets sighting fish.
>
> You were a sacrificial object
> on which your fellows
> (it seems to
> me) offloaded their burden of sin;
> they cared nothing
> for the harm
> that half a season left you dumb.
>
> But you revealed something else to me—
> my knowledge of you was different,
> I experienced the tender side of you,
> which was warmth
> and an elegant tongue;
> you were trapped in a condition
> from which I learned that men repay
> art and tenderness
> with derision
> and I did not lose from being warned
> that a man's reward is not his measure.
> . . . The day before yesterday you died;
> they let you out by the window;
> bareheaded
> they raised you on high—
> you had a place and respect at last.
>
> <p align="right">(<i>trans.</i> Donald MacAulay)</p>

This seems to me to be a profound and interesting poem, dealing with the negative side of the community, that is the conservative side which will not allow for the particularities of the individual. The person in this poem is a sacrifice to the community, he represents the human cost of keeping the community in balance, he is the scapegoat which keeps the community healthy. And there is no disguising the fact that we find this in all communities, nor, transposed, is it all that different from the treatment a Solzhenitsyn would receive from a larger one. The writer of the poem understands the person who is the sacrifice because he belongs to his own world, that is the world of art and elegance. The community sometimes inflicts an inhuman justice which is revealed in the lines

> And I did not lose from being warned
> that a man's reward is not his measure.

The closing lines are, however, the most subtle and the most interesting (the line "they let you out by the window" refers to perhaps the narrowness of the doors in the island house). The ironic fact is that the mourners now respect the "sacrificed one" when he is dead, by taking off their hats. They are now able to fit him into a safe ritual which they were unable to do when he was alive. The poem suggests the danger of the community which tends to see people as types rather than as individuals, as comforming, or not, to an unspoken ideology. When he should perhaps have been raised on high when he was alive, it is only death that exalts him now, safe, unthreatening death. And, paradoxically enough, his ideas divorced from his personality may posthumously move the community forward, which they cannot do while he is still alive.

There is no point in romanticising the community for that would be to withdraw into the dream, to deny the existence of envy and jealousy, to refuse to live in a world inhabited by real people. In fact the principle we are concerned with here is on balance the same as we see in the life history of anyone considered a rebel, or "different," as is underlined by MacAulay in another poem about an artist, Pasternak. The poem is entitled "Pasternak for Example" and the imagery used is, as is common with MacAulay, drawn from the community which he himself knew and knows.

> You winnow in a contrary wind
> living seed out of beard and chaff,
> since you have understood that those who hated you
> did not recognise
> your love:
> you prepare seed for planting
> since you have understood their inadequacy—
> that they consign all seed for milling.
>
> (*trans.* Donald MacAulay)

Again in his usual subtle manner MacAulay has realised that it is precisely the sacrifice who may have the greatest love for his community, in the sense that he sees its shortcomings and wishes to make it more perfect. The community, however, can only see that love as hate and the individual as hostile and threatening.

MacAulay's poetry seems to me to be a relevant and highly intelligent critique of the idea of the community by an exceptionally sensitive and complicated man who has himself grown up within a community. Nor should this be taken to imply that he has abandoned the community but rather that he sees its possible dangers.

Derick Thomson, unlike MacAulay, sees a possible solution for the broken community in Scottish Nationalism, while not, however, being blindly dogmatic. In a number of poems he is concerned with the forces that have almost irretrievably ruined island and Highland society, as for instance in his poems "The Herring Girls" and "Strathnaver." He will not, however, accept Scottish Nationalism as a panacea which will heal all wounds, allowing us all to remain passive.

> Envy will not,
> grudging won't,
> slanging can't prepare the ground.
> "I myself,"
> "My own clan,"
> "My class" are bandages, I've found.
> Neither priest
> nor presbyter
> nor church can say for us the creed.
> New boats will not,
> nor will looms,
> oil won't give us what we need,
> till a new redeemer comes—
> Sir Harpsichord MacGillybums?
>
> (from "The Plough," *trans.* Derick Thomson)

It is true that we have to be very careful when reading Thomson's poetry, for it is often possessed by a wicked irony. Thomson places the responsibility on the shoulders of the Scots themselves—"our own cross on our own shoulder-blades." And in a sense beyond economics, beyond the oil, there it must rest: decisions must be taken open-eyed in a real world which will not give presents without contradictions.

A more resonant poem which arises from the pathos of inner history is "Water and Peats and Oats":

"Water and peats and oats"—
a word in a stranger's mouth,
in the throng of the town,
in the town of the strangers.
Madness. The foolish heart
lapping along these ancient rocks
as though there were no sea-journey in the world
but that one.
The heart tied to a tethering post, round upon round of the rope
till it grows short,
and the mind free.
I bought its freedom dearly.

(trans. Derick Thomson)

It is this continual brooding on the home which separates the island poet from the English poet, but which may bring him closer to the European poet. It is precisely the incomplete and wavering nature of that home which sets the tongue under the tooth, which makes the poet probe his exile like a diseased tooth. To begin freely from home and colonise experience is a luxury that the modern islander does not have. It is this doubleness we find in much of Thomson's poetry, as in "The Second Island":

> When we reached the island
> it was evening
> and we were at peace,
> the sun lying down
> under the sea's quilt
> and the dream beginning anew.
>
> But in the morning
> we tossed the cover aside
> and in that white light
> saw a loch in the island,
> and an island in the loch,
> and we recognised
> that the dream had moved away from us again.
>
> The stepping-stones are chancy
> to the second island,
> the stone totters
> that guards the berries,
> the rowan withers,
> we have lost now the scent of the honeysuckle.

(trans. Derick Thomson)

This is not to say that the idea of the community is a negative one. Take this poem called "Cotriona Mhòr":

> Your picture is at the back of my mind
> undimmed,
> steady, set
> among the broken images,
> amid the movements,
> untouched by age except the age you were,
> the great round of the face like a clock stopped
> on a Spring morning,
> keeping me to the village time
> with that wisdom
> that flourished without books,
> with the fun, the cleverness-with-words
> that leapt from the heart of the race
> before it was encased,
> before it had the new valve in it
> to keep it going in the new world.
> That is the key to my museum,
> the record on which I play my folklore,
> the trowel with which I turn the ground
> of the age that is now gone,
> the image that keeps control over false images.
>
> *(trans.* Derick Thomson)

Here we have a portrait of a character who belongs to the village. She is set in her wisdom against the mechanical movement of the "outer" world. She is the guarantee that keeps control of the "false images." As often in Thomson, wisdom is contrasted with the knowledge derived from books, for this kind of wisdom is that which is reflected back from the character of the community. Books on the other hand are the works of individuals produced for individuals. Yet the pathos of the poem lies to a great extent in the fact that the music of this world cannot return in the mechanism which threatens it. Nevertheless the picture is ultimately an affirmative one, dominated by the wisdom of the woman whom the poet so much admired.

Another characteristic of Thomson's poetry is the immediate sensuousness with which he can evoke the world from which he has come, and he sometimes does this in terms of feminine imagery, as in "I Lost my Heart to You":

> I lost my heart to you at the start of May,
> your thighs were warm,
> firm and smooth, and though you were a maid

> your breasts were full,
> beautiful beneath green satin;
> and in the lambs' month June
> I lay upon you,
> and you were not defiled;
> and when July came
> the buds of the plants burst open
> and bloom came on the cotton grass;
> but then came anxiety
> and tears on cheeks,
> and before I knew what to say
> a brown tint spread over the bracken,
> and I could not say—I had not the heart to do it—
> that I had lost the smooth silk of the cotton grass.
>
> (*trans.* Derick Thomson)

Sometimes he thinks of the island as a mother:

> The child's way is difficult to forget,
> he rubs himself against his mother . . .

In a long poem called "In the Vicinity of Hol" this sensuousness emerges in detailed pictures:

> the cat warming himself
> where the stone was hottest: the lambs leaping
> without knowledge of the snow . . .

or

> The boys playing hide-and-seek among the cornstacks
> with the merry heart of evening, and a wind from the sea
> stroking their thighs and backs with a piercing ache.

It is observable that here too Thomson refers dismissively to books:

> and I think at times it was not my task
> to be reading books and scraping with a pen
> but to be alive entirely on the food of the eye . . .

His collection *Between Summer and Autumn* is full of this immediacy. Look, though, at the opening poem of the book, called "Clouds":

> Waxed bandage on my eye, so that I do not see how you have changed, dark island, long missed.
>
> Though I left light-heartedly, in youth's brashness and gaiety, my eye on a distant horizon, my steps hurrying towards it,

The horizon was only the cloud-base; cloud after cloud quenched the sparkle, of the sun on the sea I wanted, of the phosphorescent gleam in my heart.

Cloud piling on cloud, tricking me daily, Barvas Hills before me, Mèalaiseal in a blue bloom.

Little Mùirneag across the loch, as though I could touch it with an oar, the Silver Mount to the south—I need not feel depressed.

Bayble Hill beside me here, and Hòl crouching to the north—but I went away from them, on a tether, as far as love goes from hate.

(trans. Derick Thomson)

Part of the reason why I have quoted so much from these writers is that they are not known by many of those who write about the islands, and it seems to me that points can be made more easily by choosing from among the most truthful and sensitive spirits of the islanders, and where better to look than in poetry, where truth is imperative? It is true that in the past, and even now, there are poems drawn from within the community itself which reflect back on the community as they emerge from it, but to choose from writers who are themselves "exiles" is to show that it is not only the facile ceilidh that is to be found in the city. Whereas the latter is an attempt to freeze experience and time itself, the poem on the other hand, as it is articulated by these writers, is an attempt at diagnosis, at analysis, at a real living study of the effects exile can have on highly gifted individuals. It is with a sense of shock and shame that we see such energies continually breaking as at an invisible Culloden of the spirit, perpetually falling back on elegy, when they should be building from confident axioms. Part of the intention of this essay is to diagnose the disease which causes this paralysis. Behind the haze of falsity imposed on the islands, both by outsiders and naïve exiles, lies the brokenness which will not allow writers the confidence that others can have, who when they write do not feel their subject matter disappearing before their eyes.

And indeed transposed into another culture we find the heartbreaking agony of a MacAulay poem describing, with the irony only an islander can feel, the anguish of the other islander as "servant." The poem is called "Navigation":

> He comes down
> every day
> to where we lie on the beach

stretched out.
He circles us first
taking his time
and then if we're in good form
he eases his bonnet
and blesses the time of day.

He points out with his finger
where the boat sits
empty
gently rolling
its prow beached on the sand:
he raises his hand to the sky
making plain
the benefits derived on such a day
from sailing
on a cool sea.

With light step for an eighty year old
his trousers rolled to the knee
he goes out
grabs an oar
and stands and waits—
an old man who in his life
has learned good manners
and patience—
and who practises cunning.

(trans. Donald MacAulay)

Thus when we consider community and the island experience we recognise that it is not nearly as simple as it looks. Nevertheless it can be said that if the laws of history had been different, community can be considered as having more positive than negative aspects. If we were to take an extreme case, it would be worse to be set in the void of New York, than to be set in a community, even though that community may be a hostile one. It may be the case that Solzhenitsyn, by leaving his community and entering another one, is more deeply unhappy than he would have been if he had stayed. For at least criticism from within the community gives one's life purpose and a possible future.

To work harmoniously within an accepting community must be as high a pleasure as is known to man, and the greatest periods in art, as in other activities, occur when this happens. One of the problems of modern man is that he does not have a real home, and for the modern writer that he does not have a real audience, only individuals scattered here and there, pin-points of light answering each other from space. It is hard for a writer to surrender those resonances of home which speak of a lived past, stones which are memorials to incidents and experiences. Wordsworth, a very wise writer, saw this clearly and indeed "Michael" is a key text for exile and home and alienation, and readily understood by an islander.

The problem of language is, one supposes, the most important one that faces the person who analyses his own experience in the islands, for it is in many ways central to an island experience. As I have already said, for the islander to lose his language utterly would be to lose, to a great extent, the meaning of his life, and to become a member of a sordid colony on the edge of an imperialist world.

The history of Gaelic shows alternating patterns of attack and neglect. There was a period when the language was banned in schools, and when I was growing up there was no Gaelic spoken in the village school even by teachers who were Gaelic-speaking. It was as if an English child were to be taught in French by Englishmen, and to have first to learn French before he could become educated at all.

I cannot now remember how I learnt English after coming to school: Gaelic became a subject on the curriculum in the same way as Physics, or Chemistry, or French. When I entered the secondary school in Stornoway I had to repeat my first year (though I had already done my first year in the village school) because French was compulsory in the secondary school and I had learnt none in the village school. This seems to me, looking back on it now, a bizarre situation and even at the time it was one I resented.

There is no question that a language holds a community together in its various manifestations, and that to have to learn a new language in order to be educated at all is a dangerous and potentially fatal attack on that community and those who form part of it. For the imperialist language is imperiously and contemptuously degrading the native one. Because English is associated with so many of the important concerns of the real world, including education, and because English is the language spoken by "important" people such as doctors, many of them incomers, there rises a deep and subtle feeling that English must be superior to Gaelic, thus consigning the Gaelic speaker to the status of a peasant as the Anglo-Saxon was under the Franco-Normans.

The Gaelic speaker feels himself to be inferior, and his language inferior. He begins to think, for instance, that English literature is more important than Gaelic, that as a cutting instrument for getting on in the "world" English is more valuable than Gaelic, and that since English is the language of the upper classes it has a real relationship to status and promotion. He is doing exactly what the ambitious

Anglo-Saxon did when confronted by Norman imperialism. Thus we find that the language is betrayed by those who live within it and that those who propagandise for Gaelic are considered by a strange paradox to be cranks, eccentrics on the edge of the "real" world, whereas it is they who are reacting against an unnatural situation. It is as if the Anglo-Saxon, by resenting Norman mastery, were showing himself to be unreasonable whereas in fact he was being essentially and naturally reasonable.

What is forgotten is that a language and its traditions are not by any magical transformation made into more important ones as if by absolute and necessary law. There is nothing in English, for the islander, which is superior to Gaelic except in the sense that he has been made to believe that the English world must be presumed to be more important than his own since it deals with "real" issues. Nevertheless for most people the real issues are not those of politics but rather those which are the same everywhere: how they will earn their daily bread, how they are to live. No one world has a greater "reality" than another: language can be used as an instrument of imperialism but the world that it creates is not by definition a better, more important one.

For the writer, for instance, it is not a good thing to be writing in a language which is not truly his own. Nor is it the case that he should accept that English literature is in some sense superior to Gaelic literature. For the person who lives inside that literature, Gaelic literature has its own resources, its own riches, its own way of reflecting the world; and the poems I have quoted, though often constrained by elegiac reflection, show that Gaelic literature can produce work of great consequence. This is done at a cost. Some years ago I wrote a play in Gaelic about the Trojan War and it was felt by some that this was not a suitable topic for a Gaelic writer. I disagreed, and still disagree. There is no reason why the Gaelic writer, if he wishes, should not comment on ideas and events which transcended the Gaelic world. In other words the Gaelic writer should write about the Vietnam War, if he wants to, in exactly the same way as E. M. Forster could write about India. The obstacle is not in principle a real one, it only arises from an inverted principle which has been imposed on the Gaelic world by outsiders: and the islander should not accept such propaganda which does not have the welfare of the language at heart. Why should the Gaelic writer accept the idea that only other writers have access to the treasury of the global past, and that it is not his job to comment on the "real" world?

This is wrong and can be shown to be wrong—just look at how Sorley MacLean, the Gaelic poet, can deal with the outside world, and do so in great poetry as he did in his poems about the Spanish Civil

War. There is no reason why Sorley MacLean should not have felt as deeply about the Spanish Civil War as Auden did, and indeed MacLean could see in the imperialism of Franco a reflection of the imperialism which had imposed itself on Highland history.

MacLean's poems about the Spanish Civil War or about the war in Africa in the Second World War are as good as, and in most cases better than, those by writers who wrote about them in English. The following poem, "The Choice," marries uniquely the love tradition of Gaelic poetry and its balladic intensity with the new material presented by the Spanish Civil War.

> I walked with my reason
> out beside the sea.
> We were together but it was
> keeping a little distance from me.
>
> Then it turned saying:
> is it true you heard
> that your favourite white love
> is getting married early on Monday?
>
> I checked the heart that was rising
> in my torn swift breast
> and I said: most likely;
> why should I lie about it?
>
> How should I think that I would grab
> the radiant golden star,
> that I would catch it and put it
> prudently in my pocket?
>
> I did not take a cross's death
> in the hard extremity of Spain
> and how then should I expect
> the one new prize of fate?
>
> I followed only a way
> that was small, mean, low, dry, lukewarm,
> and how then should I meet
> the thunderbolt of love?
>
> But if I had the choice again
> and stood on that headland,
> I would leap from heaven or hell
> with a whole spirit and heart.
>
> (*trans.* Sorley MacLean)

Indeed, quite as clearly as Auden did, MacLean sees the close relationship between human and political choice and understands that every choice is in a deep way political. It was precisely because of his adherence to the Gaelic tradition that MacLean became a great poet and it was precisely because of his adherence to the Scottish tradition that MacDiarmid became a great poet. It was, for instance, because of this adherence to a Gaelic tradition that MacLean was able to write such a powerful poem as "Death Valley," about the war in Africa:

> Sitting dead in "Death Valley"
> below the Ruweisat Ridge
> a boy with his forelock down about his cheek
> and his face slate-grey;
>
> I thought of the right and the joy
> that he got from his Fuehrer,
> of falling in the field of slaughter
> to rise no more;
>
> of the pomp and the fame
> that he had, not alone,
> though he was the most piteous to see
> in a valley gone to seed
>
> with flies about grey corpses
> on a dun sand
> dirty yellow and full of the rubbish
> and fragments of battle.
>
> Was the boy of the band
> who abused the Jews
> and Communists, or of the greater
> band of those
>
> led, from the beginning of generations,
> unwillingly to the trial
> and mad delirium of every war
> for the sake of rulers?
>
> Whatever his desire or mishap,
> his innocence or malignity,
> he showed no pleasure in his death
> below the Ruweisat Ridge.
>
> (trans. Sorley MacLean)

There is a directness in that poem, almost a simplicity, which English poetry of the time hardly achieves. The last verse seems to me to have a justice based on the tradition of the best Gaelic poetry, since the best Gaelic poetry has always been direct and not ornamental or "misty." Indeed in another of his poems about the war in Africa, MacLean can write an elegy for a very brave but not physically imposing English soldier, comparing him to a great Gaelic hero, Alasdair of Glengarry.

It is true that Gaelic poetry does not, like English poetry, have resources of stylistically articulated irony on a large scale and that the Gaelic poet has not, on the whole, been an artist in the same way as many English poets and writers have been. This does not mean that Gaelic poetry is without its own individual power, as shown in the wrought massiveness of the love poetry of William Ross or the Old Testament vindictiveness of Iain Lom. And it seems to me that the Gaelic poetry of today is at least as great as any in the past and is able to deploy greater resources.

If we are to believe in choices then I believe it is our duty to keep clear and facing on the reality another window which is the Gaelic window, and not because that window is quaintly shaped or that behind it we see quaint people and quaint scenery but because we see through it, as elsewhere, the glories and malice and envies and subtleties of mankind. Behind the neglect of Gaelic and behind the neglect shown to Highlanders is the idea that their world is doomed by history, that it has nothing to say to us now that "progress" is leaving it behind. As if anyone who knows anything about the twentieth century could believe this for a moment, for if the Nazis were progressive where would that leave the inhabitants of the Gaelic world? And if the roots of Nazism were not in themselves in the twentieth century, what can one say of a MacLean fighting to defend a disappearing native culture in the deserts of Africa?

The ironies proliferate. And it was MacLean's great achievement that beyond this progress he saw deeper, into the life and death of an individual human being, the dead German soldier seen so clearly with his forelock down about his cheek in the tangled grave of ideology. There is no way in which the Gaelic world can be shown to be inferior to any other, any more than the Nazis could show except by pseudo-scientific theory that the Jew was inferior to the German. In essence, to dismis the Highlander as being inferior is to make the same mistake as Hitler did: that is, not to see the Highlander as human and real but as a stereotype, a comic target and not an individual with his own feelings.

The island world has been one of exile and disorientation in the terrors of history, and it should be the aim of the government to give it help and sympathy. A confident island world secure in its own language and its own values would be of significance to the state. If money is to be poured endlessly into the British motor industry, for example, is there no money to keep a whole culture alive? There is no question of saying that money alone will solve the problem but that it would help is evident, and that the British people should take an interest in such a culture would be of the highest significance.

History is not always allowed to happen: if that were the case what is the meaning of Salamis and the battle fought against the Spanish Armada? If one were to argue that economics must take care of businesses and cultures then exactly the same argument as might be used against the Highlands and Islands can be used against the British motor industry. Why is it that the British motor industry must be protected against the power and self-confidence of another stronger culture? One could say, if the argument were to be accepted, that in the "real" world of today the British motor industry is an anachronism and that the Darwinian theory of survival of the fittest should take care of it. But we do not say this, for history is not inevitable.

There seems to me to be no alternative to the proposition that Gaelic-speaking children should be taught in their own language when they first go to school, and that to impose English on children at that age is, and must be, damaging: to go from the colloquial world of the village and into the formal world of education, to go from one language to another where the school is the castle which by its language dominates the surrounding countryside, must be a blow to the psyche, an insult to the brain. To grow up inside a fixed language is a privilege which the islander has not had in recent centuries: he is in fact, and must be, the divided man in the very depths of his consciousness.

Nor should it be beyond the will of the government to propagandise in the opposite direction, to say that it is an addition to the health of a country that such a culture should exist, and freely exist. Deliberate wilfulness on the part of certain members of Parliament in the Gaelic debate on Donald Stewart's Bill made it appear as if the Gaelic language were embarking on an imperialist course and trying to impose itself on Scotland, a notion which is ludicrous.

To remove Gaelic and its speakers from the "real" world must be to inflict damage on that world whether it realises it or not. The urban world which so many inhabit is not in itself an attractive one, and it is quite possible that the contradictions in society itself are so deep that it may not be able to supply its own people with the necessities of life. Nor will anyone be satisfied with the impression of sordidness that he gets from travelling through British cities, the breakdown of transport, the graffiti which shows the aggression of the "homeless," the language of hatred, ferocious and misspelt, the feeling that one has of an urban world breaking down: the rushing from late trains to vandalised telephones, as if this was a land where people no longer feel at home.

Such a world is not progress, it is the sick turning-back of progress itself, for the uprooted are taking revenge on society by turning against it and writing on walls the grotesque language which is the reality that lies deeply beneath the contradictions of schools and other institutions. Where is the home of the urban dweller now? And if he looks into his mind what does he see but images of aggression and violence, beggary and greed, hatred and envy? One stands at railway stations and stares at West Indian ticket collectors, wreathed in filthy smoke, looking furtive and hunted, without pride.

It is against such a failure that one can set the idea of community, the idea of a culture, and who would care to say that the islanders have turned their backs on a world that is viable and worth preserving?

It is possible that far from the world of the islands being archaic it is a model of a world which might return, though not exactly in the same form. The individual cannot go on forever bearing his alienation and abstraction: for if he will not find a true community then he will find a false one, like the National Front or some other organisation. For it is clear that the returning exiles who may appear comic are searching for that which they have not found, meaning a home, materialism having left them in the middle of the wood in darkness.

The attack on the island world both internally and externally was based on the values of materialism, and now that the possessions and treasures have receded, perhaps forever, such a criticism might seem at the least short-sighted. To learn French in order to enter the ranks of the unemployed is a real paradox.

To write like this is not to join the Eden dream, for Eden never existed in society and was never part of history. To write like this is merely to say that there are and were elements in the island community that are of the greatest value; that we should nourish such elements where we can find them. Though I have admitted that there are imperfections in the idea of community, as in every other human form of society, I know that I would rather have been brought up in Lewis than in the vast derelict areas of some of our cities.

If the island world were securely based then much of the guilt that the islander feels in making his choices would be removed. It would be possible for the islander to leave his island if he wished and still prosper without guilt in another place. It is, I think, interesting that Derick Thomson has translated two poems by Solzhenitsyn in his book *Freedom and the Eagle* (1977), because he sees that the island problem is, in fact, a universal problem. Do the Russians allow their inhabitants to leave Russia without guilt? If that were so then Russia would be a confident society. There is no real comparison between two such societies in the sense of compulsion and oppression, but there is a deep connection which has to do with exile and love.

It seems to me that as I travel through Britain, as I often do, what I see is a plea for a home, for a name, for attention. It is this that island society has been seeking from the outside world, though in its own community such things are possible and do exist.

In a society which is still concerned with class to a great extent, it is important to say that the community in which I grew up was a classless one. It is possible that, seen from the outside, the islanders might be characterised as belonging to a peasant society. Seen from the inside, however, the islander does not think of himself as a peasant nor does he consider himself as being set in a particular social scale. Indeed questions of that nature have never really troubled him, and when I myself first read the works of the Angry Young Men—and especially those of Osborne—I did not feel that this had any meaning for me. It was later, when I first encountered some of the members of what may be called the English Southern Belt, that I recognised class at all, and was shocked by it, for to believe that a man or woman can be labelled according to income and school seems to me an abomination of the human spirit.

It is true that the islander looked up to the schoolmaster and the minister and indeed, certainly in the past, would cut the minister's peats without taking payment. But the reason why they looked up to these men had nothing to do with class. It was a recognition of their usefulness to the community. Education in particular was respected, not as a method of climbing out of one's class but, to a far greater extent than is common nowadays, for its own sake.

The criterion in such a society always was, not what class does such or such a man belong to, but can he do the things that are necessary? Is he a good fisherman, is he a good teacher, is he a good crofter, can he cut peats, can he tar his house? And, as I already remarked, the word *cliù* is inextricably connected with the community as such. The idea of honour or fame, as concerning above all individual achievement unrelated to community, was not a worthwhile one. Those who had *cliù* were those who conformed to the *mores* of the society and its ideals. The film star who has a high reputation but is morally tainted would not in such a society have *cliù*. The moral parameters were inextricably intertwined with the social ones.

It was I think the case that one might not be able to conform to the demands of such a society, firstly, if one's life were morally unacceptable and, secondly, if one could not carry out the practical tasks that were the common ones. The loneliest people in such a society would be the impractical people. When one considers the attacks made on the islanders for laziness and inefficiency it would certainly be worthwhile to point to their versatility, their ability, for instance, to build their own houses without expert help.

As one who was not himself practical I admired this versatility greatly, and sometimes my admiration transcended itself and became astonishment. It is true that to be impractical was to be an internal exile and also might lead to a certain a mount of ribbing. However, it is possible that such an impractical person might have some other gift to bring to the communal treasury: he might, for example, be a good singer or a good storyteller or he might have a sharp wit. And again this wit was not a "peasant-like" wit but reached a high degree of sophistication. We are not dealing here with a dull, peasant-like society but rather with a highly intelligent one which sees quite clearly what is going on around it and can draw its own conclusions.

True, the islander has an innate courtesy and a lack of aggressive sense which above all is disgusted by any show of grandiosity. He finds it difficult to put himself forward—as if by the act of doing so he was individualising himself from the community—and for this very reason he can tolerate manifest unfairness with a patience that is often long-suffering.

I am not concerned here with a scientific analysis of the islander's character such as one might find in a book of sociology, but rather with describing in an impressionistic manner a society as I found it myself. Such a society is not interested in the aesthetic in any real sense. It has been said, for instance, that the standard of singers in the Highlands is not high but this, however, is to judge the singing in a wrong way. Angus Macleod, a Gaelic singer, sang with great fervour, in a voice from which notes emerged like solid boulders. In my opinion he sang certain songs most lovingly. No purist would ever be able to convince me that Macleod's singing was not beautiful and powerful: the passion of the singing, the solidity of the notes, appealed to a profound resonance in my own nature, and was thus for me the highest pitch to which singing could attain.

The islander, as I have said, is not concerned with the aesthetic for its own sake and is not interested much in modern poetry, some of which does not appeal directly to his own experience—thus it might very well be the case that the poetry of Donald MacAulay or Derick Thomson would not be the sort that he would read. But at the same time he knows what he requires in singer and poet, and that is genuine feeling related to his own concerns. It is true that this might lead to the acceptance of songs which are essentially sentimental—and many of these songs are about the islands themselves—but that this demand for genuineness is a real one cannot reasonably be denied.

The islander too is not greatly interested in the theatre for the simple reason that in the past he has not been used to one. It is significant, however, that when a play like *The Cheviot The Stag and The Black Black Oil* was shown in island halls it made a great impact. A sparse community will naturally be concerned with issues which closely affect it. In a sense too the poetry of such a society will be characterised as "naïve" in the highly specialised sense that it is not ironically or artistically articulate but will be a response to an event or a situation.

This is a real society in a real world and it will therefore be characterised by the particular reality to which it belongs. To have a strong grasp of that which is around one and to be able to deal with it is surely a virtue: but we do not get the individual brilliances which are characteristic of the urban world and for which much has to be paid. Such individual excellence as we do have is usually exported. It is to be remembered that the poetry of a Baudelaire emerges out of an alienation and loneliness which, humanly speaking, are hard coinage to expend.

The poetry that is best liked will emerge from that society itself and will incorporate its values while even making superficial fun of them: and it must be said that it is unusual to find elsewhere in Britain (except perhaps in Wales) a society in which bards are common, the historians in verse of their villages. Nevertheless a wholly radical attack on the values of such a society would be met with hostility, whether coming from inside or from outside.

The comprehensive nature of education has always meant that a class structure will be absent, and that indeed a concept like class, as has already been said, is wholly alien to such a society. I found when I visited Australia in 1980, that it is the class consciousness of, especially, the southern English which is most disliked, so that in fact the southern English do not see Australia at all as a country with its own indigenous laws, its own indigenous literature. (It is rather like the Claude mirror which gentlemen tourists used to carry about with them in the eighteenth century in order to impose on actual nature the picture of "real" nature which had been sanctioned by art.)

Similarly, Gaelic literature is not seen at all, though we get editions of other literatures, from all continents of the world. It is as if Gaelic literature does not exist. There are in Gaelic literature poems of the highest achievement characterised, however, by concerns and patterns which may not be precisely those of, for example, English literature, and at their best are passionate, lyrical and intense. The idea, however, that life imitates art would be alien to the spirit of

Gaelic literature and even inconceivable. The dandyism of an Oscar Wilde with its close associations with class would immediately be sensed as false. Genuineness is what is demanded of Gaelic literature and though this may lead at times to sentimentality, sentimentalism itself has to be more clearly defined than it has been in the past for one to accept critiques of it without examination.

As I have already said, I can well understand why the poems of a false Eden arose. They are the products of a lost home. If English poetry were to emerge from the "lost home," it too would be sentimental: a settled society can produce great poetry, and since the nineteenth century especially Highland society has not been settled. The poetry of personal loss is, however, a different matter and who is to say that Hardy is more poignant than the anonymous writer of the following lines:

> If Seathan could be but redeemed
> the ransom would be got like rushes,
> the silver would be got like ashes,
> gold would come from the edge of the meadows,
> wine would flow like the spring water,
> beer would be got like a cool verdant stream;

or the later ones in the same poem:

> O Seathan my brightness of the sun!
> alas! despite me death has wholly seized thee,
> and that has left me sad and tearful,
> lamenting bitterly that thou art gone;
> and if all the clerics say is true
> that there is a Hell and a Heaven,
> my share of Heaven—it is my welcome to death—
> for a night with my darling,
> with my spouse, brown haired Seathan.
>
> (*trans.* Alexander Carmichael)

Sincerity is a concept which needs refining and studying. In a sense the poetry of exile is sincere. In a sense the poetry that one sees in "In Memoriam" columns in newspapers is sincere. The problem is that poetry of this nature may appear false, exaggerated, and thin. It might, however, be worthwhile to quote here a comment in a review from *Aquarius* on *The Collected Poems of Gavin Ewart*:

> These poems eloquently confute again and again the title of one of the last in this collection, "How Tragedy is Impossible." He does a companion poem entitled "How Life Is Too Sentimental"

which, describing his own and his wife's feelings on the death of their child, finishes with the lines:

> And the word 'sentimental'
> has come to mean exaggerated feelings.
> It would have been hard to exaggerate our feelings then.

As it would have been hard to exaggerate the feelings of those who by necessity were forced to leave their homes and write:

> The moon brings to my mind
> the many nights we were together

followed by the later lines:

> You my love are dearer to me
> than my mother who reared me when I was young.

Such deep feeling, however, can lead to pathos as in the lines:

> Shawbost is most beautiful to me
> where I was reared when I was young,
> where are the peatstacks . . .

One of my most surrealistic experiences was to stand once on the deck of a ship sailing to Lewis and hearing an English voice say, "I shall be glad to get home to Bayble" (my own village), and I remembered then that there were many people who never got home to Bayble, among them relatives of my own, no matter how much they might have wished to do so. At that moment was I being chauvinistic, sentimental, unfair? I don't know. The complex of ironies glittered too brightly for me to feel anything other than a sense of desolation combined with the free laughter of the comic which is so closely related to the tragic.

For in such a society contradictions must always abound, and there are so many others that cannot be listed here: and associated with these contradictions are innumerable guilts, the guilt for instance which I myself often feel when I recall that when I was studying at Aberdeen University my mother would have been gutting herring in Yarmouth. It is easy for me to write a poem saying that the blood which I shed in my poetry is like the blood which ran from her gloves on those cold foreign mornings and in that salty light; but that is not sufficient, for it is not an aesthetic fact, nor can it be resolved aesthetically, that one should have to leave home at such an age to do a job like the gutting of herring so far from one's own home.

For these reasons I have been always suspicious of the glitteringly aesthetic. Metaphor can sometimes be used to conceal insoluble contradictions in life, and Yeats's poem "Easter 1916" did not solve the Irish crisis, it only clarified it. In the end society lives and works outside the metaphor, and to think that the metaphor solves anything except the problems set by the poet would be silly and unrealistic. Beyond the poems of Seamus Heaney, beautiful though they are, the masked men will stand above the draped coffins saluting an empty heaven with their guns.

It is almost as if one wishes that a debt should be paid to the islanders for their exile, and here I shall give a brief portrait of an uncle of mine who became one. At the age of sixteen he ran away to join the Army and later he sailed to Canada. (It was not perhaps with regard to this particular ship that sailed from Stornoway that my mother told me the story of the emigrants leaving after the First World War. As they stood at the railings of the crowded ship they and the people on the shore sang together in Gaelic the words of the Old Hundredth, that music of pathos drifting across the water and the many ironies that separated them.)

My uncle worked building railways, and sometimes did not work at all, and slept in dosshouses where shoes had to be nailed to the floor lest they be stolen during the night. His underwear, like that of his friends, was at last in rags. Many of them died of drink, others starved. He was lucky, eventually reaching Vancouver where he became a Fire Officer at the end of his journey. Latterly he would fly to Lewis, even at eighty years of age, and every week read the *Stornoway Gazette* which he had sent to him from home. When I saw him, and later in Nova Scotia I saw the Scottish names familiarising the exiles with their lost homes, when in Australia I heard of Highland exiles who had drifted into hopelessness and alcohol, I was angered by the waste, the dreadful waste of our island humanity. We are owed—such men are owed—not indifference but at least understanding and care. It is not right that a whole culture should have been treated in this way, that like the Red Indians and the aborigines so many of our people should have had to leave their homes to inherit the worst aspects of a so-called superior civilisation.

People should have a right to a stable home, to their own language, they have a right that work should be provided for them in exactly the same way as British Leyland had work provided. It is not as if the Highlander is lazy or inefficient but, as everyone knows from his own experience, only hope can provide the resilience that life demands. It is as if behind the criticism that is made of them is the idea that they are somehow sheltering from history, who have seen so much of it, far more than the bureaucrats in their offices.

I recall the stormy days on which the islanders went out fishing, when fishing was available. I recall those who left my village in the last war, so many of them to be drowned in foreign seas which they had only seen previously in geography books. I recall the numbers of young boys who were lost from my own village, and perhaps I might recall those who were truly sheltered in bureaucratic offices. I recall the tragedy of the *Iolaire* when over two hundred sailors were drowned a mile from Stornoway, on a New Year's morning when their wives and children were waiting to celebrate their return. I recall reading of the forlorn carts which carried dolls from the wrecked ship into the town, presents for the drowned men's families. It is not surprising that nostalgia should be their sickness, that from their masts they should remember their disappearing village.

I think of them in Canada hacking down the dark tall trees, clearing away spruce so that they could plant. I recall both the successful and the unsuccessful, the latter who never wrote home because there was nothing to write about. I recall the broken ones who returned. And it is as if a terrible anger seizes me when I think of the many dead, the waste.

There are many who wish to stay in the islands. They wish to stay there just as everyone wishes to stay in his home. They wish to stay there because there they are surrounded by familiar resonances. But how is it possible for them to do so when unemployment is so high, when they who have so very little money have to spend more on their necessities than those who are closer to the heart of civilisation. "The qualities of the islander are those which are not suited to the modern world"—thus the given impression. They are not suited because the islander is in general honest, law-abiding, modest in asking for rights which should be human rights. If the qualities demanded of modern civilisation are slickness, greed, willingness to get away with what one can at whatever cost, aggressiveness and even violence, then the islander is not civilised. And this is not to fall into the trap of the eternal Eden, for it is historically the case that he is law-abiding—one hardly ever hears of a serious crime taking place on the islands—and even in drink the typical islander is not violent and more likely rather to relapse into melancholy and gloom than to strike out aggressively. Indeed one of the most extraordinary sights I have ever seen was a saloon bar on an island boat with islanders singing not drunken travesties of secular songs but rather psalms, and this not mockingly but with passion and dedication and purity.

I recall the fishermen sending fish round the houses in my youth. I recall the way in which the sick were looked after, how the rest of the community would help them with their peats and other domestic needs. I recall the dances at the end of the road on the autumn nights when there was a reddish moon in the sky and nothing could be heard but the music of the melodeon and the sound of the sea. And I shall not be accused of belonging to the dream when I have already mentioned the flaws which are to be found in the community as in any human organisation. We are not concerned here with a poem but with a life which, though hard, was not bitter.

I recall with a sense of injustice my own fragmented life, the choices I had to make when I didn't realise that I was making them, the losses I endured before I well knew that I was enduring them, the contradictions I was involved in before I knew they existed. And I know that my own life has been a snake pit of contradictions, because of an accident of geography and a hostile history. I envy, for instance, those poets who have developed in a stable society, who can start from there and are not constantly analysing the very bases of their art.

It is no accident that religion—sometimes too extreme in my opinion—has gained power in some of the islands, since if there is nothing much in this life then surely there might be something in a future one. Nor is it surprising that one of the "gifts" of this religion has been a weakening of the will, a fatalism of the kind that George Campbell Hay in a conscious comparison sees both in the Highlander and the Arab. Nor has Derick Thomson been silent about it either when in "The Eagle" he writes:

> "It is good to have a touch of the eagle in us
> though the lamb's lot is better,
> authority is good
> though it is good for the soul to submit,
> it is good to take wing
> though comfortable to be in a fold"—
> that at any rate is that the eagle-priest said
> reading holy writ from the book of stone.
>
> (*trans.* Derick Thomson)

Or later when in "The Journey" he writes of the drunkard:

> Returning to Lewis,
> my heart full with pleasure,
> I thought of that first sight
> of the Shiant Islands,
> Park and Kebbock Head appearing,
> and the mouth of Loch Ranish,
> Point and the Castle Grounds,
> but I missed them in the Bar,
> I was so full of joy.
>
> That week at home
> there was no time to get sober,

> I was plastered from dawn to dusk—
> I never saw the Barvas Hills this time—
> I was as happy as a dog in its own dump.
>
> And the day I left,
> what homesickness!
> I took a burst in the Royal,
> and if I got aboard I must have slept;
> didn't know what to say
> When Ullapool Pier came in sight.
>
> Lord God,
> when will I see you again, Mount Sion?
>
> <div align="right">(<i>trans.</i> Derick Thomson)</div>

And Sorley MacLean writes with much anger in "A Highland Woman":

> Hast Thou seen her, great Jew,
> who art called the One Son of God?
> Hast Thou seen on Thy way the like of her
> labouring in the distant vineyard?
>
> The load of fruits on her back,
> a bitter sweat on brow and cheek,
> and the clay basin heavy on the back
> of her bent poor wretched head.
>
> Thou hast not seen her, Son of the carpenter,
> who art called the King of Glory,
> among the rugged western shores
> in the sweat of her food's creel.
>
> This Spring and last Spring
> and every twenty Springs from the beginning,
> she has carried the cold seaweed
> for her children's food and the castle's reward.
>
> And every twenty Autumns gone
> she has lost the golden summer of her bloom,
> and the Black Labour has ploughed the furrow
> across the white smoothness of her forehead.
>
> And Thy gentle church has spoken
> about the lost state of her miserable soul,
> and the unremitting toil has lowered
> her body to a black peace in a grave.

> And her time has gone like a black sludge
> seeping through the thatch of a poor dwelling:
> the hard Black Labour was her inheritance;
> grey is her sleep to-night.
>
> *(trans.* Sorley MacLean)

Now it is no wonder that the islanders have turned to the church, for the church at least offers stability in a shifting world. Nor is it any wonder that one of the archetypal figures among the islanders is the exile who has lived a drunken life abroad and who when he returns home becomes the inveterate churchgoer with the hard bowler hat and the watch chain. When he is abandoned to the waves he is saved by a grasp more rigid than normal: he becomes a statue in his own land, a harsh stony one. If humanity could not save him, God must.

For one like myself who is not committed to any ideology, whatever religion it comes from, whatever demands it makes (and these usually at the expense of the human), the church, and some churches more than others, is alien, though it perhaps creates an illusion of steadiness at the expense of the wavering present. Certainly, as Thomson has written, when the fire was shifted from the centre of the floor it became the internal fire of hell, and a real living community of folk story and poem was replaced by one held together by the bonds of a fixed creed. The secular poem became sinful and the psalm took its place, as seen for example in the poem "Gospel 1955" by Donald MacAulay:

> I was at the meeting last night;
> the house was full, packed to the door,
> there was no place for me to sit
> but a cramped nook on the stairs.
>
> I listened to the psalm: the tune
> transporting us on a tide
> as mysterious as Maol Duin's;
> I listened to the prayer
> a liberating cascading melody—
> my people's access to poetry.
>
> *(trans.* Donald MacAulay)

If we should mock the rigidities of such a religion we must also remember that rigidity is the price one pays for insecurity: if there is no real home then an unreal one will be provided. And I have seen some of my own friends, from fear and guilt, entering that world of religion to gain the peace which may have to do with life eternal but has little to do with the chanciness and loveliness of life as it is daily lived. If they were once condemned to shaky ships now they are condemned to a darkness which masquerades as light. If the light of the city was too dazzling for them in the individualism which rose like a sharp rock from communion, then another communion has taken its place. It is always to the human consequences that we must look, and while the church has offered something to the islands—a sort of hope which is a substitute for a greater despair—it is a condemnation of history and its agents that such a rigid shelter should have been necessary.

In all honesty, we should be asking those who have remained, "Why did you do so?" And we should not simply answer, as many do, by saying, "Of course if alternatives had been open to them, they would not have remained." In all honesty we should not be dealing with the exceptions, with those who are crucified by the contradictions, with those who feel the guilt of desertion. We are not dealing with those who, while remaining in the city, look forward each year to the joyful, unthinking return. We are not dealing with the artists, the guilty and gifted ones. We are to ask those who remain a naked, direct question, "Why do you stay?" And they stay, I believe, firstly because this is their home no matter how many attempts have been made to diminish it. And also because they feel themselves as belonging to a community which has always been there. There are among them those who have travelled the world and returned, not because of a dream but because this is the life they wish to lead, a life where everyone is known to everyone else, where the consequences of the daily round are visible, where the landscape is their landscape and where they have not disowned their dead, where there is no rampant individualism, where their surroundings though often bleak are their own.

We all know of those who refuse to leave the slums of Glasgow for new council houses. They were not happy to leave because they belonged to a human community which, whatever their surroundings, at least gave them the warmth of companionship, instead of the windy bare acres of council schemes. They were deeply and profoundly and instinctively right, for only the exceptional individual like a Columbus will set out on strange seas facing the world anew each day, trembling but still moving forward. And while not condoning slums, much of the unrest and aggressiveness that one feels almost palpably in cities arose from the shifting of whole populations to grey and uncolonised wastes. Should it not be considered reasonable to keep rootedness in being wherever possible? For the unrooted person, unhappy and alienated, will turn in a frenzy against those buildings which do not belong to him, which stand up against him and outside him as the death of the spirit, the very heart of hopelessness. Deeper than any disease that society suffers from is the sense of the lost home, the ugliness of the new one, the destruction of community. And when we see the policemen advancing in Brixton with their shields, is it not against those who have not found a home to replace the one which they have lost?

To grow up on an island is a special experience, but it is not an experience of Eden. Newspapers arrive late, the world outside is distant, its concerns are remote. Above all there is the sound of the sea, that eternal sound that haunts the islands, and has found its commemoration in a poem which is, like so many of our poems, an elegy. It is called "The Eternal Swelling of the Sea":

> The eternal swelling of the sea,
> listen to its high boisterous noise.
> As it was in my youth
> is the great sound of the seas,
> pitiless, unchanged,
> mixing the sand of the shore,
> the eternal swelling of the sea,
> listen to its high boisterous roar.
>
> Each wave with its crest
> restless, sonorous, white,
> with imperious haste
> surly, plumed, unafraid.
> But its speed will be checked
> at the brink where the other ones died
> as the people have gone
> who once in this town would reside.
>
> In the woods of the west
> I'd never desire to stay.
> My mind and my wish
> were to set on this loveable bay.
> For those who were kind
> in deed and friendship and joy
> are scattered like birds
> whom their enemy seeks to destroy.
>
> Willows and rushes
> thistles and sea-bent and grass,
> have choked all the springs
> where once I would drink to my wish:
> and the walls are now cold,
> by groundsel and grass made infirm,
> and the nettle is red
> and tall round the hearth that was warm.

> As I now look round
> how should I not suffer grief?
> For the people are gone
> whose badge was friendship and love.
> Poor exiles, they've been
> pursued across the salt seas.
> Never more will they hear
> their high swelling thunderous noise.
>
> But I must depart.
> No more shall I walk in this place.
> My age and my hue
> reveal how short are my days,
> and when I am swathed
> in the chillness of death and its sleep
> prepare my last bed
> by the high-swelling roar of the deep.
>
> (trans. Iain Crichton Smith)

It is true, of course, that this is a sentimental poem, but that it contains a profound sense of loss is also evident.

The forces of economics are driving the present population out of the islands. How much longer can high unemployment and increasing freight charges permit them to remain where they are? And when this happens will it not represent a diminution in the riches of Britain? It is easy to say that islanders are responsible for themselves, but how can this be applied to those whom history has treated so badly? How is it possible to tell a man to get up when his legs have been removed?

There is no question in my mind that a society which lives by materialistic values will be destroyed by them. If materialism has not been accepted by Western society as a philosophical concept then it has accepted it as the force by which it lives. The great powers are, to a larger extent than one is often willing to accept, mirror images of each other. I do not think that the opposite of materialism is another inflexible concept but rather those motions of the spirit which see the human being as he is, whoever he is, and really notice him. That materialism, naked and unashamed, has come to rest in Britain is a fact, however we choose to disguise it. That that belief in materialism is closely connected with the destruction of community is also, I am sure, a fact, for materialism depends on individuals being set over against each other. It is now much more difficult to see the human being as he is without the armour of money or achievement. Sometimes when I walk the streets of Glasgow I see old women passing by, bowed down with shopping bags, and I ask myself, "What force made this woman what she is? What is her history?" It is the holiness of the person we have lost, the holiness of life itself, the inexplicable mystery and wonder of it, its strangeness, its tenderness.

If this respect for the human being, unmoneyed, without status, is lost, how can a society stand except as a mockery of what life ought to be in its most precious essence? If the justification that the islanders should continue to exist or leave be a purely material one, then nothing can be done to save the culture which they represent and which they inherited. If, however, we are to prove our superiority to those forces that stand over against us, we must make sure that we are not infected by the vices of those very forces. Our alternative must be a real alternative. It must be an alternative which shows sensitivity, which treats men with care, which really sees them. How else will we not be involved in the contradictions of history? The greatest moment in our recent history was when we stood out against the bestialities of Nazism and in defence of the human being because in our deepest natures we were outraged by the maltreatment of him. At such moments man takes on the righteous holiness which in spite of all else and beyond ideology is a radiance in his nature. If we do not remember that reliance on materialism is the death of a civilisation as surely as the barbarians have been, then we are lost. It is on sensitivity that the future of this particular culture rests, that the future of any culture rests: not indeed to mark out this particular culture as a reserve but to help where it needs help, to grant it the possibility of a future; and not to be put off by its independences and its obstinacies any more than we would by the cantankerousness of any individual.

Honesty must now admit that we are at the point of the greatest decision with regard to the islands and to the language. The forces attacking it are more and more dominant. Television is perhaps the most frightening force of all, since its heroes compel admiration from the young. More and more we see that the poems which are written now are elegiac, their endings turned in on themselves:

> And my country's artists
> give tongue like migratory geese,

and

> I thought of the grave that I had a care for
> in the cold country to the north

and

> O transient flower
> O world that is gone

and

> Neither talk nor tea will heal this pain.

There is a possibility of saving that culture if those who have been converted by internal imperialism, and those who have only external imperialism, were to realise that its extinction would be the death of a precious thing. If instead of consigning this culture to the oblivion of history people were to say, "You are necessary," that would be sufficient encouragement for living. If people were to say, "We recognise you for what you are, we know your life history, we see you,. we know your name," then something might still be salvaged.

To live is to be conscious of a history. No man can live if every action taken, no matter how enthusiastically, runs eventually into the sand. To give such a culture the possibility of a future means that the children must grow up in a world that they recognise as being as important as any other. It means that they be not divided into two by the sudden incursion of a new language. It requires that the artist should sense a future and not be forever imprisoned in the forms of the elegiac. It requires not derision but respect. It requires a government that is concerned for all its people including those who speak a language that they do not understand.

It is not the case that there are no leaders in such a community, but leadership in turn requires that men act in a real world and that the results of their actions are visible in a real world. One of the poems that I have already quoted delineates clearly enough one of the results of the lack of such a future, and that is drunkenness, exactly the response that is made among societies which are derided and diminished by stronger ones. It is easy enough, as Compton Mackenzie has shown, to transform whisky into the eternal colours of the comic, as if the islanders were children, but the matter is much more serious than that. And it is not enough for the church to attack drunkenness, as if it were a manifestation without source, for very often the drunkenness, among other things, is a subterranean attack on the church itself and its inflexible rigidity. It is also the response of a man to a reality that excludes him, it is the response of a man who sees himself as irrelevant to history. In Chekhov's plays we read of the superfluous man, one who sees history passing him by, and who catches sight now and again of the flicker of new flames on the horizon. And yet history is not an inevitable machine. The English mariners who set out against the Armada did not believe in the inevitability of history, nor did the Greeks who combed each other's hair at Salamis. To say that history is inevitable is to submit to the creed of those whom we oppose. History is not a natural force like electricity.

History is composed of decisions. It is unfortunate that the Calvinism of the islands is an ideology that weakens the will and complicates even more a situation that is still salvageable. When I consider a Britain that is without the Welsh and Gaelic communities I consider a Britain that would be, at the very least, less interesting than it is at the moment. When I see on bookstalls at airports and railway stations throughout the world the same books and magazines, I see a world that is boring and without depth. We are told this is the direction that History will take and must take. But I do not believe in the necessity for it. I do not believe that it is rigorous and unchangeable, beyond the manipulation of man.

And in fact we do not believe this. Not even the monetarism of Margaret Thatcher permits its own total logic, for if that were so the British car industry would not be saved time and again. Even she recognises that there are other considerations which must prevail beyond that of inevitability: and she partly recognises this because she is forced to by the power such a group might exert. If people were truly honest they would say that beyond all the arguments the reason why the islands are not helped more than they are is because they exert no power on the "real" world: and this, I think, is in fact to admit the justice of the very ideas that she is opposing. We attack a society that prevents the conditions of the Jews being made better (as in Russia). When the islander sees that the laws of humanity are not applied in his own case, why should he feel patriotic towards a country that abandons him to the detritus of history? What were the friends of my youth fighting for in the last war? Were they fighting for the disappearance of their own land? It is this point which is made by John Smith (1848-81) when he writes in his poem "The Spirit of Charity":

> Does anyone remember
> in this age the bitter day
> of that horrific battle,
> Waterloo with its red plains?
> The Gaels won doughty victory
> when they marshalled under arms;
> when faced with strong men's ardour
> our fierce foes had to yield.
>
> What solace had the fathers
> of the heroes who won fame?
> Their houses, warm with kindliness,
> were in ruins round their ears;
> their sons were on the battlefield
> saving a rueless land,
> their mothers' state was piteous
> with their houses burnt like coal.

While Britain was rejoicing
they spent their time in grief.
In the country that had reared them,
no shelter from the wind;
the grey strands of their hair were tossed
by the cold breeze of the glen,
there were tears upon their cheeks
and cold dew on their heads.

(*trans.* Derick Thomson)

And when one considers the multiple ironies of making Stornoway a NATO base one is staggered and bemused. What exactly is this NATO base defending? Is it defending the values of materialism which denuded the islands themselves? Is it defending the many exiles who have already left? Is it defending us against opposing mirror images of materialism? And this in the very centre of a religion which converts life itself into rigidity: truly the roundabouts of history are salt with irony. For from these denuded islands will fly planes which will defend us against those who are, it is said, attacking the Jews for clinging to their own culture instead of to a larger more imperialistic one. No wonder that deep in the hearts of the islanders, in their very bones, must resound the laughter of the absurd. In these dizzying multitudes of ironies the mind is lost and confused: one is bewildered by the spectacle of friends of one's youth drowning in seas which they only knew as belonging to a globe inhabiting a classroom in which they were taught in an alien language by those who could themselves speak Gaelic.

This essay is concerned with the contradictions that one person has found inside a culture. The trouble with many of the books about the islanders is that they have been written from the outside, and no matter how much these writers may investigate and speculate, they do not feel these contradictions in their bones. They do not, for example, feel the contradictions of the academic who has to go to Glasgow or Edinburgh or Aberdeen to teach his own language in a university. They do not understand what it is like to be in a city while teaching that subject and speaking English for the most part. They do not understand what it is like to have to make a choice as to whether to teach Gaelic to his children who grow up and are part of that environment and to whom Gaelic is an alien language as much as it is to their English-speaking peers.

They do not understand the contradictions between the economic direction of a life and its cultural one; the Highland academic, for instance, who marries a woman from outside the Gaelic world. They do not understand the academic's possible attitude to the "ceilidh," which is one of the few methods of keeping Gaelic alive in the city. They do not understand the weight of guilt such a person might bear. In other words, they do not understand the waste which accompanies the choices.

Such questions seem to me to be the real ones, but they can only be fully lived out by the islander himself, and they are so complicated that they are hard to write about and he can even feel ashamed of them. Thomson is, I think, the poet who has brought out most clearly this feeling of betrayal and helplessness, as in "Coffins":

> A tall thin man
> with a short beard,
> and a plane in his hand:
> whenever I pass
> a joiner's shop in the city,
> and the scent of sawdust comes to my nostrils,
> memories return of that place,
> with the coffins,
> the hammers and nails,
> saws and chisels,
> and my grandfather, bent,
> planing shavings
> from a thin, bare plank.
>
> Before I knew what death was;
> or had any notion, a glimmering
> of the darkness, a whisper of the stillness.
> And when I stood at his grave,
> on a cold Spring day, not a thought
> came to me of the coffins
> he had made for others:
> I merely wanted home
> where there would be talk, and tea, and warmth.
>
> And in the other school also,
> where the joiners of the mind were planing,
> I never noticed the coffins,
> though they were sitting all round me;
> I did not recognise the English braid,
> the Lowland varnish being applied to the wood,
> I did not read the words on the brass,
> I did not understand that my race was dying.
> Until the cold wind of this Spring came
> to plane the heart;
> until I felt the nails piercing me,
> and neither tea nor talk will heal the pain.
>
> (trans. Derick Thomson)

Implicit in the poem is the idea that the betrayal was taking place inside a childish ignorance, that choices were being made without the child's even knowing about them. Consciousness appears when the options are closed.

One of the most interesting things that has been happening recently, however, is the return of their natural leaders to the islands, in order to exercise the control of practical affairs that has often in the past been lost to others. These are people who have gone back to take part in the Bilingual Project (in Lewis), to run the local radio. But unless more is done for the islander, especially with regard to the most significant arm of the media, that is, television, it may be that such a sacrifice will not be enough.

One feels like a Hercules around whom prolific hydras are spawning. When one head is cut off another rises, and one runs round the arena in continual activity. And the trouble is that these monstrous heads are both internal and external. Why not give up altogether, someone might say; what is the point of this resistance? But there is something irretrievably necessary in the work that is being done, for it is recognised, however consciously or unconsciously, that a language in a deep sense is inextricably intertwined with what one really is and that the loss of it would be not only a diminution but a death. Would it not be the same for an Englishman, would he not also feel that if he ceased to speak English he would no longer be the same person, but, like a character in Chekhov, appear superfluous? And was not the antagonism between Tolstoy and Turgenev, the former even challenging the latter to a duel, a real antagonism with real issues at stake, issues which went beyond the literary? And no matter how much we may admire Nabokov's talent, can we not say that he is a writer at play, dealing only with dilettantish enigmas? Conrad is a specific case whose grandeur is more difficult to analyse except to say that he created a nautical community of his own. Time and time again we come back to the language as the ultimate justification for the culture, and we may ask what such a language has produced in literature to justify our admiration for it. And the answer is that it has produced a great deal. I have already shown that this is true of the modern poets who exist on the edge of elegy, but when one examines the poetry of the language we can see there poems as profound in their own way as those of the English culture, as, for instance, the poems of Duncan Ban MacIntyre, to choose only one poet whose nature poetry is in its innermost heart different from that of the English, not philosophical at all, but clear and hard and musical and strongly visual at the same time, as in "Ben Dorain." And this kind of visual hardness which is so evident in "Ben Dorain" is a particularly obvious quality in Gaelic poetry down the centuries, as in these lines from a seventeenth-century poem:

> I see the red lips turned black,
> and the chalk white teeth turned to black bone

or the lines:

> You took the east from me, you took the west from me,
> you took the moon from me, you took the sun above,
> you took the heart from me, from out my breast,
> you almost took my God from me, my white love

> Badger's blood on your shirt,
> and deer's blood on your coat

It is in "Ben Dorain," however, that we find the truly sunny joy of Gaelic poetry with its fidelity of observation and its subtle variations:

> Pleasant to me rising
> at morning
> to see them the horizon
> adorning.
>
> Seeing them so clear,
> my simple-headed deer
> modestly appear
> in their joyousness.
>
> They freely exercise
> their sweet and level cries.
> From bodies trim and terse,
> hear their bellowing.
>
> A badger of a hind
> wallows in a pond.
> Her capricious mind
> has such vagaries!
>
> How they fill the parish
> with their chorus
> sweeter than fine Irish
> tunes glorious.
>
> More tuneful than all art
> the music of the hart
> eloquent, alert,
> on Ben Dorain.

The stag with his own call
struck from his breast wall—
you'll hear him mile on mile
at his scale-making.

The sweet harmonious hind—
with her calf behind—
elaborates the wind
with her music.

Palpitant bright eye
without squint in it.
Lash below the brow,
guide and regulant.

Walker quick and grave,
so elegant to move
ahead of that great drove
when accelerant.

There's no flaw in your step,
there's all law in your leap,
there's no rust or sleep
in your motion there.

Lengthening your stride,
intent on what's ahead,
who of live or dead
could outrace you?

The hind is on the heath
where she ought to be.
Her delicate sweet mouth
feeding tenderly.

Stool-bent and sweet grass
the finest food there is
that puts fat and grease
on her flanks and sides.

Transparent springs that nurse
the modest water cress—
no foreign wines surpass
these as drink for her.

Sorrel grass and sedge
that grow on heath and ridge,
these are what you judge
as hors d'oeuvres for you.

Luxuries for does
between grasses,
St John's wort, the primrose,
and daisies.

The spotted water-cress
with forked and spiky gloss;
water where it grows
so abundantly.

This is the good food
that animates their blood
and circulates as bread
in hard famine-time.

That would fatten their
bodies to a clear
shimmer, rich and rare,
without clumsiness.

That was the neat herd
in the twilight,
suave and trim, unblurred
in that violet!

However long the night
you would be safe and right
snug at the hill's foot
till the morning came.

The herds of the neat deer
are where they always were
on the wide kind moor
and the heathland.

When colour changed their skins
my love was most intense,
they came not by mischance
to Ben Dorain.

(*trans.* Iain Crichton Smith)

In its combination of tenderness, sunniness, music and observation and knowledge of subject matter we hardly find this kind of poem in English at all. Yet other languages are translated into English and the poetry of this part of the world is ignored, as if nothing worthwhile could emerge from the Celtic races. Truly the Gaelic speakers are invisible in Britain, all knowledge of them confined to films which show them as pawky, loveable and ultimately distant (like the black servants in Hollywood films). In an age where women are seen as a race different from men, where children too are enfranchised, the inhabitants of parts of this island are not seen at all, as if they did not exist, as if their language were rather like the grunts Red Indians make before setting off against the cavalry of Hollywood. Even Samuel Johnson took a far more intelligent interest in them than anyone does now.

So that one can sometimes feel like that beggar I saw in Aberdeen with the pennies beside him in his cap, black glasses over his eyes, vulnerable and open to the day. It is as if we were saying in the end—"All we can look for is justice. All we can look for is the sensitivity that will not pass by, that will pause and study, that will sense in the inmost heart the unfairness of the desolation of a culture. These ships broken by history should be seen as bearing a precious and valuable cargo. The destruction is not complete, the last chance is not lost. Much help is sent to foreign lands, yet so little is given to those inhabitants of our own."

I should like to end with a poem of my own which I have translated from the Gaelic. It is called "Shall Gaelic Die?"

(1)

A picture has no grammar. It has neither evil nor good. It has only colour, say orange or mauve.
Can Picasso change a minister? Did he make a sermon into a bull? Did heaven rise from his brush? Who saw a church that is orange? In a world like a picture, a world without language, would your mind go astray, lost among objects?

(2)

Advertisements in neon, lighting and going out, "Shall it . . . shall it . . . Shall Gaelic . . . shall it . . . shall Gaelic . . . die?

(3)

Words rise out of the country. They are around us. In every month in the year we are surrounded by words.
Spring has its own dictionary, its leaves are turning in the sharp wind of March, which opens the shops.
Autumn has its own dictionary, the brown words lying on the bottom of the loch, asleep for a season.
Winter has its own dictionary, the words are a blizzard building a tower of Babel. Its grammar is like snow.
Between the words the wild-cat looks sharply across a No-Man's-Land, artillery of the Imagination.

(4)

They built a house with stones. They put windows in the house, and doors. They filled the room with furniture and the beards of thistles.
They looked out of the house on a Highland world, the flowers, the glens, distant Glasgow on fire.
They built a barometer of history.
Inch after inch, they suffered the stings of suffering.
Strangers entered the house, and they left.
But now, who is looking out with an altered gaze? What does he see? What has he got in his hand? A string of words.

(5)

He who loses his language loses his world. The Highlander who loses his language loses his world.
The space ship that goes astray among planets loses the world.
In an orange world how would you know orange? In a world without evil how would you know good?
Wittgenstein is in the middle of his world. He is like a spider. The flies come to him. 'Cuan' and 'coill' rising.*
When Wittgenstein dies, his world dies.
The thistle bends to the earth. The earth is tired of it.

(6)

I came with a 'sobhrach' in my mouth. He came with a 'primrose.' A 'primrose by the river's brim.' Between the two languages, the word 'sobhrach' turned to 'primrose.'
Behind the two words, a Roman said 'prima rosa.'
The 'sobhrach' or the 'primrose' was in our hands. Its reasons belonged to us.

(7)

'That thing about which you cannot speak, be silent about it.'
Was there a pianist before a piano? Did Plato have a melodeon?
Melodeon in the heavens? Feet dancing in the heavens? Red lips and black hair? Was there a melodeon in the heavens? A skeleton of notes.

(8)

'Shall Gaelic die?' A hundred years from now who will say these words? Who will say, 'Co their?'** Who? The voice of the owl.

---

* 'Cuan' means 'sea' and 'coill' means 'wood.'
** 'Co their?'—'Who will say?'

(9)

If I say 'an orange church' will I build an orange church?
If I say 'a mauve minister' will I create him?
The tartan is in its own country.
The tartan is a language.
A Campbell is different from a Macdonald (this is what a tartan teaches).
The tartans fight each other. Is that why they had to put a colourless church between them?

(10)

Said Alexander Macdonald, 'It was Gaelic that Adam and Eve spoke in that garden.' Did God speak Gaelic as well, when he told them about the apple? And when they left that garden, were they like exiles sailing to . . . Canada?

(11)

Shall Gaelic die! What that means is: shall we die?

(12)

An orange church with green walls. A picture on a wall showing ships like triangles. On another wall, a picture of a cafe with men made of paint. 'Gloria Deo' in the language of paintings, an orange bell, a yellow halo around the pulpit where there are red dancers.

(13)

Were you ever in a maze? Its language fits your language. Its roads fit the roads of your head. If you cannot get out of the language you cannot get out of the maze. Its roads reflect your language. O for a higher language, like a hawk in the sky, that can see the roads, that can see their end, like God who built the roads, our General Wade. The roads of the Highlands fit the roads of our language.

(14)

When the ape descended from the trees he changed his language. He put away the green leaves. He made small sharp words, words made of stones.

(15)

The dove returned to Noah with a word in his mouth.

(16)

The scholar is sitting with a candle in front of him. He is construing words. He is building a dictionary. Little by little, inch by inch, he is building a dictionary. Outside the window the children are shouting, a ball is rising to the sky, a girl and a boy are walking without language to bed. What will he do when the ball enters the quiet room, breaking the window, stopping him at B, and Z so distant.

(17)

Whom have you got in the net? Who is rising with green eyes, with a helmet, who is in the net?
Cuchulain is in the net, he is rising from the sea, ropes of moonlight at his heels, ropes of language.

(18)

'When you turn your back on the door, does the door exist?' said Berkeley, the Irishman who was alive in the soul.
When the Highlands loses its language, will there be a Highlands, said I, with my two coats, losing, perhaps, the two.

(19)

A million colours are better than one colour, if they are different. A million men are better than one man if they are different. Keep out of the factory, O man, you are not a robot. It wasn't a factory that made your language—it made you.

(20)

Like a rainbow, like crayons, spectrum of beautiful languages. The one-language descended like a church—like a blanket, like mist.

(21)

God is outside language, standing on a perch. He crows now and again. Who hears him? If there is a God let him emanate from the language, a perfume emanating from the dew of the morning, from the various-coloured flowers.

(22)

Death is outside the language. The end of language is beyond language. Wittgenstein didn't speak after his death. What language would he speak? In what language would you say, 'Fhuair a' Ghaidhlig bas?'*

---

* 'Fhuair a' Ghaidhlig bas'—'Gaelic is dead.'

(23)

When the name 'Adam' was called, he turned his back on the hills. He saw his shadow at his feet—he drew his breath.

(24)

You cannot say, 'Not-Adam.' You cannot say, 'Not-Eve.' The apple has a name as well. It is in the story.

(25)

The gold is new. It will not rust. 'Immutable universal,' as the Frenchman said. But the pennies, the pounds, the half-crowns, these coins that are old and dirty, the notes that are wrinkled like old faces, they are coping with time; to these I give my allegiance, to these I owe honour, the sweetness. 'Immutable, perfect,' Midas with his coat of gold and of death.

It is not a witticism to say "Shall Gaelic die?" What that means is "Shall we die?" For on the day that I go home to the island and speak to my neighbour in English it is not only the language that has died but in a sense the two who no longer speak it. We would be elegies on the face of the earth, empty and without substance. We would not represent anything, and the world would be an orphan about us.

I imagine those who lose their language dying in the same way as the language dies, spiritless, without pride. One imagines the tourist then entering a world which would truly be inferior to his own. One imagines the beggars of the spirit, no longer real people in a real place. They will be shadows cast by an imperialistic language that is not their own. For if they speak a language that is not their own they are slaves in the very centre of themselves. They will have been colonised completely at the centre of the spirit, they will be dead, exiles, not abroad but in their own land, which will not reflect back the names they have given it. Such a people will be a race of shadows and in that final silence there will be no creativity. They will be superfluous, talking without alternative in a language that is not their own.

—Written in 1982: previously unpublished.

Part Two

The Poet's World

Between Sea and Moor

Brought up on the island of Lewis, I never left it till I was seventeen years old and went to Aberdeen University. When I think of Lewis now, when I try to feel it again in my bones and flesh, what returns to me?

The moor and the sea.

I could never live away from the sea. Days when it drowsed in the sun, when among rank flowers we sat on a headland and watched the ships sailing by. Days when the rain streamed down the window panes and the sea was grey and dull about the bare island out in the bay.

Days when the waves were playful about the rocks. Days when I used to draw drifters with crayons on a page of writing pad. Days when we used to search for crabs among the pools or sit on the pier swinging our legs, watching the faint blue hills across the water.

Days in Stornoway when, a pupil at the Nicolson Institute, I would walk along the quay watching the drifters with their orange buoys and men seated, apparently sewing, among green netting. Salt in the nostrils. Herring in barrels. The grey shops crouched facing the sea and the masts.

Nights of astonishing silence when the moonlight laid yellow roads across the water.

Many years afterwards I would think of my mother working as a fishergirl among those barrels, wearing her flesh-coloured gloves, an inconceivable girl in a world so different from mine, and I would feel guilty as if I had condemned her to that life.

The sea, monster and creator, has remained with me as a well of fertile symbolism. I think of the many dead—some I have known—drifting about in it, being refined there forever. One of the best footballers in the island was drowned there one terrible night. Another boy was blinded by an oar. The *Iolaire* sank there on New Year's morning, in 1919, bringing home from the war two hundred men to be drowned on their own doorsteps, a tragedy that breaks the mind. And yet on summer days how innocent it looks, how playful, how almost Mediterranean. How easily like a human being it is transformed from serenity to anger, from calm to sudden outbursts of rage. On an island the sea is always present. Always one hears the sound of it behind the painted day, a background, a resonance, the loved and feared one.

My house lay between the sea and the moor: the moor which was often red with heather, on which one would find larks' nests, where one would gather blaeberries: the moor scarred with peatbanks, spongy underfoot: blown across by the wind (for there is no land barer than Lewis). I am a child again, barefoot, jerseyed, bare-kneed, the daisies are growing, the daffodils are a blaze of yellow. The smoke of the village chimneys is rising into the sky. There is a vague desultory hammering, dogs are barking, there are cows munching clothes on the line.

Days when we played football all day, nights when we played football by the light of the moon, returning home across the moor like sweaty ghosts, the moon a gold football in the sky.

How can one be that boy again? How can one walk home from the well with the two pails brimming with water, on paths that are probably now gone, between the cornfields, and through the long wet grass?

The moor and the grass and the sea. Throwing stones at telegraph poles, jumping rivers, watching roofs being tarred, hearing the lazy hammering of stones from the quarry.

The sky of Lewis above the stones, the sea, the bleak landscape almost without distraction of colour.

And beyond it all on moonlit nights hearing the music of the accordion and the feet of the dancers from the end of the road, having thoughts of a warm eternity brooded over as by a hen with red feathers.

Later, but in Dumbarton, I would try to write about some of this in a complex of images which I called "Some Days Were Running Legs":

> Some days were running legs and joy
> and old men telling tomorrow would be
> a fine day surely: for sky was red
> at setting of sun between the hills.
>
> Some nights were parting at the gates
> with day's companions: and dew falling
> on heads clear of ambition except light
> returning and throwing stones at sticks.
>
> Some days were rain flooding forever the green
> pasture: and horses turning to the wind
> bare smooth backs. The toothed rocks rising
> sharp and grey out of the ancient sea.

Some nights were shawling mirrors lest the lightning
strike with the eel's speed out of the storm.
Black the roman rooks came from the left squawking
and the evening flowed back around their wings.

The phrase "and old men telling tomorrow would be / a fine day surely" refers to the one indisputably marvellous day in the year. This was the one day when we—that is, my two brothers and I—were allowed to visit Stornoway, seven miles and a whole world away. On the night before, I would go and ask the old men of the village, one by one, what sort of day the following one was going to be, terrified in case it was going to rain. And the following morning, how early I got up, how I waited trembling at the side of the road, for the first sight of the bus, and then, when Stornoway appeared, could Babylon have been a more lustrous city?

Poor as we were, my mother long-widowed as she had been, she at least tried to afford us that visit.

She herself had never been to a cinema in her life but she allowed us to go. We ate ice-cream, we smelt the smell of apples, we wandered among bookshops which appeared vast to us, we ate chocolate, and if we were lucky we might arrive home with small wooden carts drawn by rampant wooden horses. And after coming out of the cinema we stalked the streets in a dazzle of heroism, guns strapped to our sides, rolling our tall boots along the grey pavements of Stornoway.

And much later I would write about the cinema and about Westerns, and about the Black Mask, Phantom and Spider, detective stories that I borrowed and the smell of whose yellow pages return to me now. For just as dearly as I loved Keats and Shelley—more dearly really—I loved that other world of cowboys and detectives in their lonely yet romantic settings.

I learned about John Dickson Carr, though not yet about Ellery Queen, who seemed to me to be the two towering geniuses of the classical detective story. And about the same time I read P. C. Wren and, of course, stories about the sea.

I read and read and read. I think I was really a very isolated child, isolated in school and perhaps in the village too: and isolated the more because I was often ill with bronchitis and sometimes with asthma. I was off school almost as often as I was there. In the long summer days I would lie in bed listening to the sounds that went on outside the house, in a dream of longing for some other world that wasn't this one, a world inhabited as much by English public schoolboys as by my own friends. My father had died of tuberculosis and my mother was terrified that I would also get the disease, so whenever I coughed

I was immediately bundled into bed with hot water bottles. Sometimes I felt so suffocated by this treatment that whenever I felt a cough coming I would go into the next room lest she should hear me. I would spend days in the attic reading *Chambers' Journal* or sitting at the window looking out across the village.

In the village school I was slow at arithmetic but good at writing essays on the slates that we used then. I lived in a state of perpetual humiliation, shy and secretive, often ill, and when I look at the class photograph that was taken then, wearing my brown jersey which my mother had knitted for me, and a tie-pin at the throat, I see a child whose eyes are heavy and almost dim with fright staring into a world which he finds threatening. Often I would wake at night thinking that I was haemorrhaging, for all around me the village was palpitant with the symptoms of tuberculosis which the young and the middle-aged were suffering from, and also dying from.

When later I attended the Nicolson Institute in Stornoway a strange almost visionary thing happened to me. I was, as I have said, very poor at arithmetic and mathematics. Then one day I went into Woolworth's and bought a puzzle book which I took home with me. I began to do the puzzles which were mostly, if I remember correctly, about differently coloured Easter eggs, and then one morning I woke up and found that I could do mathematics, and that above all I had fallen in love with geometry. From then on I would do geometry problems for pleasure and when the solution clicked so elegantly it was as good as being able to write a poem. Geometry appealed to some part of my nature which has to do with a love of order and elegance, and also to a part which has to do with a love of puzzle-solving. For this reason I only like challenging crossword puzzles. Even when I was in school I was trying to do *The Listener* crossword puzzles even though they were pretty well beyond me. The idea of elegance would later appear as the idea of grace, for instance in the following sonnet:

> And lastly I speak of the grace that musicks us
> into our accurate element till we
> go gowned at length in exact propriety.
> I speak of the glowing light along the axis
>
> of the turning earth that bears the thunderous sea
> and all the chaos that might learn to wreck us
> if the chained stars were snapped and the huge free
> leonine planets would some night attack us.
>
> I speak of the central grace, that line which is
> the genesis of geometry and of all
> that tightly bars the pacing animal.

> Around it build this house, this poem, this
> eternal guesthouse where late strangers call,
> this waiting room, this fresh hypothesis.

For many years the poem to me was to be an elegant construction, not sweaty but pure, a musical artefact composed of exact language.

One day when I was eleven years old and the weather was blue and perfect the most publicly important and significant event of my childhood happened. The Second World War broke out. I remember that even at that age politics cannot have impinged on me suddenly and without warning, for before the war began I had written in Gaelic a poem about Neville Chamberlain setting out with his umbrella to shield us from the storm about to come. Even then I must have thought of him as a comic figure. But certainly at eleven years old I did not realise what war would bring. It brought us gas masks which we had to try on, and which with my usual clumsiness I found difficulty in handling. Certainly it would bring us saccharine and whalemeat. And we would wander about the village in search of scrap metal to help the war effort.

But it did not occur to me then that it would send out long searching tentacles from vast unimaginable distances to pick off one by one a number of the older boys of the village who drowned in oceans which they had never seen except on a dusty globe in the village schoolroom. Thus died Rob on a cruiser in the Atlantic. And many others. They would appear with their kitbags home on leave for a few days, then later the telegram would come and they would never be seen again. My own brother was a lieutenant on a corvette and was later to be on a tank landing craft on D-Day. We worried about him a great deal but were also proud of him when he came home in his officer's uniform.

Nevertheless the war was in a way unreal. Nothing happened to us. No bombs fell on us. There were the RAF huts outside the village but hardly any other physical evidence apart from the blackout which protected us from the planes that never came. True, there was the Home Guard (or LDV) which my brother joined, once bringing home his rifle and taking it apart and assembling it in the kitchen in the light of the Tilley lamp, for we had no electricity. It was in fact difficult to get methylated spirits for the lamp, and that was one of the inconveniences of the war for us. Sweets practically disappeared and everything was meagrely portioned out according to coupons. But nothing happened to us except that one after one the boys of the village disappeared to distant seas and some went down with their ships (for of course they almost without exception joined the navy).

There was one radio in the village (it was called a "wireless" in those days, though it had wires) and curiously enough it was in a thatched house. Every night I would go and listen to it. It was perched up on a shelf with a white curtain around it, and before the news began the curtain was pulled aside, almost as if to reveal to us an idol speaking with a godlike voice. And certainly the voices that emerged from it sounded godlike, those of Bruce Belfrage, Joseph Macleod and John Snagge. They told us of Russian tanks chasing Germans through the snow and of convoys being attacked by U-boats. Names like Timoshenko, Voroshilov, and Rommel became as familiar as the names of the villagers. The wireless, of course, had an accumulator, and one day an old woman from the village came into the house and was told that the accumulator had gone down. "Obh, obh, obh," she said, "imagine that and all the poor boys on her." She thought it was HMS *Accumulator*!

It was odd and disquieting to sit in that thatched house and listen to the news, for one might hear of a ship on which one of the village boys was serving. One of the most ominous phrases that remain with me to this day is the one that the announcer would use, "The next of kin have been informed." The war looked as if it would go on forever. And yet, strangely enough, it never occurred to me that we would lose it. It was like being in a theatre watching a play which had little to do with oneself, but which one knew in advance would have a happy ending.

The village became a world of old men and women and girls. All the older boys had suddenly left. In the school itself we were mostly taught by women. In my fifth year I found myself on the magazine committee and was soundly lectured by an English teacher for having written a parody of *In Memoriam* such as one might read in the local newspaper. Girls suddenly flowered into one's consciousness in their white blouses and gym shorts. Dido and Aeneas and their blazing love affair was projected as if onto a Lewis screen. The Latin master, a ball of fire and energy, would stride into the room and without pausing would say, "Begin translating at line 567" or whatever. The Gaelic poet William Ross died of his love affair in a dusty room on a summer afternoon. And there was a perpetual hunt for French irregular verbs. That was what happened in the daytime. At night there was the thunder of guns in the deserts of Libya while Tobruk was captured, lost, recaptured.

Lewis was of course a bare island without a theatre, ballet, museums. There was a good library, however, and there I would sit during the dinner hour reading magazines like *The Tatler* bound in leather covers and seeing pictures of the aristocracy joined together by a "common joke." One afternoon I got so engrossed in the magazine that I forgot to return to school until three o'clock and was saved from punishment by a very understanding lady teacher. I think that I liked the Nicolson very much. I became reasonably good at passing examinations. I even tried the Aberdeen University Bursary Competition in fifth year and won a minor bursary, although I had great difficulty with the Latin paper since all the "u"s had been printed as "v"s and at first I wondered whether I had been given a Hindustani paper.

I moved between two worlds—the world of school and the world of the village—travelling home every night by bus. I spoke Gaelic at home and English in the school. But in those days I did not find this an extraordinary situation: I simply accepted it. I would never have dreamed of speaking English to anyone in the village, and of course most of the Stornoway people spoke only English. I was not writing much Gaelic then, only English, and what I most wrote was poems. There were no interesting Gaelic books for me to read, no adventure stories, no poetry that spoke directly to me in my own world. I used to read Penguin New Writing—though cannot now remember where I got copies of the magazine—and learned about Auden and other writers who excited me very much.

I became, I think, slightly blasé in an objectionable and rather juvenile way. I began to think of the island as constricting. I could not but see that religion was dominant and joyless, that ministers were considered as of the greatest importance, that certain people whom I despised were respected simply because they were church-goers and attended the Communions. It was as if I was searching for a wider world of ideas which I could get only through books, a freedom which I imagined as existing elsewhere. I felt myself as alienated from my own friends for I had the feeling that I was predestined to be a writer—a poet certainly—though I had not written anything that was of the slightest value. I even felt that Stornoway, which had once seemed a pulsing city, was becoming smaller and duller. I thought of the black-clad women gossiping at corners, in the biting wind, while at the same time clutching their Bibles with black elastic around them.

I would return at night from the school and do my homework—I remember mainly geometry problems and Latin—by the light of the Tilley lamp on the oil-clothed table, and I felt more and more a gap opening between me on the one side and my mother and brother on the other. So I withdrew into myself and never discussed anything that had happened in the school as if it were a secret world which I treasured and which I did not want tampered with at any cost. I did not want to have anything to do with the cutting of peats, mainly because I was clumsy, and also because I felt that such tasks were unimportant: what was important was the world of the mind. I was continually falling in love with girls who I thought were at least as beautiful as Helen, but I never told them my passion. I only dreamed about them.

The only contact I had with the boys of the village was through football, for I played outside right for the village team. I was not particularly good but I valued the games partly for their own sake but also because by means of them I felt myself part of a team, of the village itself. Sometimes if I played well I thought there was nothing in the whole world like racing down the wing with the ball at my feet, the green dewy grass below me, and the possibility of a goal ahead of me. I would listen to the radio and almost cry with frustration when in every game Scotland was hammered by a forward line composed of people like Matthews, Carter, Lawton and Finney. I could not understand why the English could keep their forward line intact throughout the whole war and thought that there must be a secret plot to keep these great and hated players available for the simple purpose of humiliating Scotland.

I had no feeling for Scotland at all as a country except through football. I did not feel myself as belonging to Scotland. I felt myself as belonging to Lewis. I had never even seen a train. I had never been out of the island in my whole life. Glasgow was as distant to me as the moon. I had hardly read any Scottish writers, not even MacDiarmid. Most of the writers I had read were English. The island was in a way self-sufficient and, strange though it seems, there were many parts of the island itself that I had never visited. For instance it was not until recently that I visited the district of Ness which is one of the most beautiful areas in Lewis. I travelled the beaten track between my village and Stornoway and it never occurred to me to go anywhere else, for hardly anyone had a car then, and we certainly did not have one. We were too poor. My mother and the three of us existed on a widow's pension of about a pound a week and most of this was spent on food. My books I got from the library or from friends, one in particular who lent me detective stories which he could afford to buy.

In a strange sort of way, too, the island seemed to have no history. There were standing stones on the moor behind our house but I never found out why they were there or who had put them there. My curiosity about the past was minimal and it never occurred to anyone to tell us anything about the history of the island. It seemed to have sprung out of the sea fully formed, scoured by the wind, brilliant in spring, with daffodils, without much animal life, and with few birds. It was a hard bleak island which did not reverberate when one touched it with one's mind.

Looking back on it now I think of its society as a very demanding one, classless, practical, and in some ways claustrophobic. One was judged by what one could do, not by one's money (for in those days very few people had much of that). The most important thing was to be practical, and I wasn't that. I have seen men from the village building their own house, which seems to me an astonishing achievement. They fished competently and did all sorts of jobs that I wished to do but could not: repairing fences, tarring roofs, cutting peats and so on.

I felt myself a dreamer in this practical world, naked and visible to it: and yet it was also a world that valued education, not just because education led to a valuable job but for its own sake too. Nevertheless, I sometimes have a nightmare in which I think that there are more teachers in Scotland than there are pupils, and I yearn for the love of ideas for their own sake: for the free play of the mind.

As I look back on what I have written I wonder: what has Lewis given me? It gave me images of the sea, and the bare mind. It gave me a respect for hard work and self-reliance and independence. It freed me from a trivial obsession with class and politics. It taught me because of my poverty not to be interested greatly in riches, and sometimes to feel that they are immoral. But I suppose that it also left me with defects, though perhaps those defects should be blamed more on myself than on my environment. It has made me, I think, unhealthily concerned with religion, so that I find I do not wholly believe in poems of the moment but rather in poems morally shaped. I find it difficult to be spontaneous and joyful in my work. There is a certain pessimism which may perhaps have to do with growing up among an ageing population, so that I seem to know more about the old than I do about the young. It gave me a respect for education from which it took me a long time to free myself, for Scottish education is simply one way of dipping into an endless sea, and that perhaps not the best one. It has given me I think a feeling for honesty and an unwholesome distrust of the Bohemian and the disorganised. The other kind of honesty that it has given me is more conventional, for there was no crime on the island. Doors could be left open and when one returned to an empty house one found that nothing had been touched. However, I do not hear coming from the island the novel cry of the transient but rather the proved monotony of the permanent. And in spite of all that, I love the island.

I love it for its very bleakness, for its very absences. I think of it as a place beaten upon by winds, an orchestra of gales, which bend the fences like the strings of a musical instrument. If it has its noises they are not supernatural ones, they are in fact the noises of our own obdurate world. And sometimes, as I have said, the island will flower into the purest dazzle of colour, the more brilliant because the more transient. One of my more recent memories is standing on a road on the moor and watching a man and woman cutting peats, bent down into the rain and wind: and then suddenly a ray of light, fugitive and serene, falling across them so that for a moment they looked as if they had been framed in a picture without glamour or glory, but rather attesting to the sudden moments of illumination or happiness that come to us out of the grind of existence.

When I was much younger I tried to put some of these ideas and feelings into a poem which I called "Poem of Lewis." I must say that this poem is a much more disillusioned one than I would perhaps write now though it has a hard, bleak truth, I hope, of its own:

> Here they have no time for the fine graces
> of poetry, unless it freely grows
> in deep compulsion, like water in the well,
> woven into the texture of the soil
> in a strong pattern. They have no rhymes
> to tailor the material of thought
> and snap the thread quickly on the tooth.
> One would have thought that this black north
> was used to lightning, crossing the sky like fish
> swift in their element. One would have thought
> the barren rock would give a value to
> the bursting flower. The two extremes,
> mourning and gaiety, meet like north and south
> in the one breast, milked by knuckled time,
> till dryness spreads across each ageing bone.
> They have no place for the fine graces
> of poetry. The great forgiving spirit of the word
> fanning its rainbow wing like a shot bird
> falls from the windy sky. The sea heaves
> in visionless anger over the cramped graves
> and the early daffodil, purer than a soul,
> is gathered into the terrible mouth of the gale.

At the age of seventeen, sometime in October 1945, I left Lewis for the first time in my life to go to Aberdeen University. I waved to my mother and brother across the space of water that separated the ship from the quay. I watched them driven away in their hired taxi and as I did so I felt as if I were saying some sort of permanent farewell. My mother suddenly looked very small and distant in her black coat and my brother withdrawn into a deep pathos of his own. I went down to my berth and slept till morning and when I went up on deck in the dawn I saw a tremendous sea spreading all around me and the sun as red as a banner in the sky. It was cold and yet I felt exhilarated.

A piper was playing on the deck. The ship sailed on through that waste of waters till we reached Kyle of Lochalsh, which seemed to consist of a flurry of seagulls above fishing boats. I went to the train which was the first that I had ever seen. All day we travelled, first through stony land and then through fertile, over which the evening sun slanted—land very different from and much richer than that of Lewis with its poor huddled crops and its stone walls.

When I arrived at Aberdeen Railway Station the first thing I saw was a beggar sitting on the pavement wearing black glasses and with a cap beside him. In the cap were some pennies. I walked into the hurrying city with my case and took a taxi to my lodgings which were opposite a statue of Byron. That night when I was lying in my bed I thought I heard someone whistling a Gaelic tune past my window, but it was not a Gaelic tune at all. When I woke in the morning I felt no homesickness, only excitement. I felt free on the anonymous streets and because I was young I found my solitude exhilarating. The granite glittered from the large stone buildings, the trams and buses passed by. I went to the University—King's College—which was anciently mellow and covered with ivy.

Lewis seemed a world away both in space and time. There were cinemas everywhere and a theatre. There were hundreds of shops, not the one shop which we had in the village. There was colour and noise everywhere. I didn't realise then that one could not leave one's childhood and youth behind so easily, as if it were forgotten luggage. And it came to me as a great surprise to hear some of the students who belonged to Aberdeen telling jokes against the city as if it were a small boring place which they wished to leave as soon as they could.

And yet years afterwards on holiday in Aberdeen from Glasgow I myself found it smaller than I had remembered. Nevertheless, I also fell in love with Aberdeen as I had done with Lewis. The moor and the granite came together in a new synthesis. And here I really began to write poetry, a great deal of it about Lewis.

—from Maurice Lindsay (ed.), *As I Remember* (1979)

A Poet in Scotland

Writing here in this room in Oban, what do I think of being "a Scottish poet"? I don't think of being a Scottish poet at all, I think of the act of writing poetry. I know that more disabling choices are available for me here—shall I write in Gaelic or in English? But at the moment of writing I do not think of these things. I say to myself, I wish there were more outlets for poetry in Scotland than there are: I wish, for instance, that there was a publishing house which would take all that I write.

All these things I think, but they are at the back of my mind when I am writing. When I have finished the poem I do not ask myself, "Is this a good Scottish poem?" I only ask myself, "Is this a good poem?" I am aware of other poets, some Scottish, some not. I am aware of the past—of so much history and fable, and some of it again is Scottish and some is not—but in the end I ask myself, "Is this a good poem?" I do not ask whether my Scottishness will save it. I know that in the end it will be in some sense Scottish because it was written by me and I live in Scotland.

And when I say I live in Scotland what I mean is that I live in a small town which has a certain Highland ambience and is different in a subtle way that I cannot define from a town on the east coast or in the south of Scotland. On the other hand, the town is really a rural one, it is not industrialised. Thus by writing here and remaining here I know that I am not dealing with "the problems of the cities." Let those who love the city deal with them. And I know that there are people who love the city but not as many here as there are Americans who love the city, as Bellow or Malamud, for example.

I know that wherever I am, wherever I go, I shall bear with me strong images from my childhood and these delimit what I am and what I shall say. I know that, in general, London poets and London literary society do not think much—if at all—about Scottish poetry, and it may be that American poets and American literary society do not think much about (or even of) English poetry. These things are on the periphery of my mind: but, I sometimes think, if only there were more respect for writing! For if one writes people seem to think that one is doing nothing, whereas they don't think that about singers, even poor singers. I know that in general there is a deafening silence round me, since the Scots are not concerned with poetry apart from that of Burns. I said "concerned," not "interested in." I know that as far as the public is concerned nothing much has changed since MacDiarmid started to write. The kailyard is the habitation of the Scot, and perhaps of the Englishman too, and perhaps even of the American. I know that even MacDiarmid, who to my mind is a very great poetic genius, will be considered as someone on the edge of things and will never enter the main channel of that sea on which literary critics brood, and which is fed by Pound and Eliot, and possibly even by Betjeman, who is not in MacDiarmid's league.

All these ideas are simmering in my mind, but when I am writing a poem I forget them. All that is important then is my poetic intelligence, my grasp of the "idea" that I am wrestling with, the person that I am at that moment, the images I possess. I know that I, too, am on the periphery of "things" and yet not on the periphery of my own world. The stones around me echo to myself and to no other, and will always do so. There is an inevitability in where I am, and that is all that concerns me. The problems are my own, as far as each poem goes: they are not Scottish. If I were other than I am, I would not write the poems that I write.

I say to myself, "It would be nice if more people read my poems." But I know that probably every poet is saying the same, whether he is American or West Indian or English.

I regret sometimes the waste of spirit involved in the choice of language. But then sometimes it is a good thing to have two languages, for I can change from one to the other and refresh myself. I can look out of two windows instead of one, and each language refreshes the other.

I am not writing for anyone in particular. I am writing to a secret command, in answer to the sudden flash of an image from a street, from a record, from a wood. Is this why I do not like poetry readings, because there I see people who actually listen to what I say, and who after all seem only to be human, when I expected gods and goddesses? Who are those earnest people, and was it for them that I wrote? No, it wasn't. I wrote because there was something I wished to make clear to myself, to commemorate, to question. For nobody, for myself—as Antigone says in the Anouilh play of the same name.

And that is how I began and that is how I shall probably continue. For if the poem feels right, that is its own justification. I do not need a democracy to judge it. I know that poetry changes nothing, and I am not interested in politics. The pain and the joy will go on forever and we exchange only one kind for another. If I have my own vanity I hope that what I write doesn't have it. If I am anxious I hope that what I write isn't anxious. Sometimes I wish I could write as well as

Lowell, at other times I wish I could write as well as Horace. My mind and my imagination may be Scottish but my reading is not wholly Scottish, nor are the poets I admire necessarily Scottish (though there are Scottish poems and poets that I admire). Essentially I am alone in front of a piece of paper. I am not surrounded by a body of echoing bards. I am fixed here in this small town on such and such a day—whether wet or dry, spring or autumn. Some mornings I think I write well and later find that I didn't. Other mornings I think I write badly and find that I wrote well. Does the plumber who goes to work in the morning wonder whether he is Scottish? And perhaps on certain days inspiration descends on him too.

On all of us, on certain days.

The world is full of poets. Everywhere they are writing and scribbling. And Scotland is only a small part of the world, and so is England. I don't wish to fix Scotland in my work nor any other land. There are difficulties but wherever one is there are difficulties, and not just for poets. For everyone. The world is never fair, to anyone. All one can do is what one most deeply wishes to do. And how many people in the world are lucky enough to do that? Or to have some obsession that gives them so much joy and so much despair, and that is, in spite of everything, a white stick in the dark.

—from Dannie Abse (ed.), *Poetry Dimension Annual: The Best Poetry of the Year* (1980)

Poetic Energy, Language and Nationhood

This obviously is a large subject and quite as obviously the only qualification I can bring to it is my experience as a practising poet and a (selfish) brooding on it. I have for a long time been interested in Edwin Muir's dictum that no Scottish poet writing in English has produced work of the first or even of the second rank and as I have a great respect for the quality of Muir's mind I focus on this paradox by which a poet condemns himself to be below the second rank (without examining too exactly what he means by the terms "first rank" and "second rank" but recognising what he means in a large and perhaps intuitive sense).

There seems to me much truth in Muir's version of Eliot's "dissociation of sensibility" when he suggests that some irretrievable damage was done to the Scottish poetic psyche, if I can use such a term, as far back as the Reformation: and I agree, too, when, for instance, he says about Carlyle in a most illuminating remark that he wrote a Scottish English and that the struggle which we sense in his prose was a peasant's struggle with an essentially alien language. And I can also see quite clearly the danger of sentimentalism which always hovers at the edge of Scottish writing, and sometimes right in the middle of it, and which has nothing to do with poetic feeling. It is one side of Burns, that side of him which was later picked up so disastrously by lesser writers: "The Cotter's Saturday Night" for instance has much to answer for.

When we read MacDiarmid's early work in English and compare it with his early work in Scots (I am thinking here of *Annals of the Five Senses* and *Sangschaw*) what we notice at once in changing from one to the other is not simply a change of language but rather an access of energy, a new freedom. One can see this very clearly, I think, by comparing the poem "The Fool" with "Crowdieknowe." What is at issue here is quite simply the feeling we have that in the second poem the poet has found himself, and that what he has found is a whole self (and this is of the greatest importance), and that that whole self allows a freer play to his whole consciousness, so that the second poem feels alive and changing, able to incorporate a queer *Scottish* (and therefore more authentic) pride and contempt in a way that the first poem is not able to do. Here is the poem "The Fool" which is written in English:

> He said that he was God.
> "We are well met," I cried.
> "I've always hoped I should
> Meet God before I died."
>
> I slew him then and cast
> His corpse into a pool
> But how I wish he had
> Indeed been God, the fool.

And here is "Crowdieknowe":

> Oh to be at Crowdieknowe
> When the last trumpet blaws,
> An' see the deid come loupin' owre
> The auld grey wa's.
>
> Muckle men wi' tousled beards,
> I grat at as a bairn,
> 'll scramble frae the croodit clay
> Wi' feck o' swearin'.
>
> An' glower at God an' a' his gang
> O' angels i' the lift
> —Thae trashy bleezin' French-like folk
> Wha gar'd them shift!
>
> Fain the weemun-folk'll seek
> To mak' them haud their row
> —*Fegs, God's no blate gin he stirs up*
> *The men o' Crowdieknowe!*

What is so startling about the change there is the access of energy we find in the second poem, the odd way in which we think of the speaker as a real person set in a real place, whereas the persona of the first poem is undifferentiated, even abstract, ego. One can hardly assign the first poem to any tradition. There is a flatness about it, a rhythmical woodenness. It might have been written by Blake except for the lack of animation. It is the poem of a poseur, a stylistic exercise. But suddenly in the second poem it is as if the poet has entered a tradition and this places his poem in its grotesquerie, its intimacy, its way of addressing God so familiarly, yet without the coldness of the persona in the first poem. Even the awkwardnesses of the second poem, "'ll scramble frae the croodit clay," help to give it authenticity.

In some strange way the language which is one's own seems to permit a freedom that is not present when one is using an alien language. No fair-minded reader can deny, I think, that what one senses above all in *Sangschaw* is a quite spectacular and marvellous delight in the language itself which MacDiarmid has discovered and which allows his consciousness total freedom in the rhythms he invents to match the inventiveness of his mind. The discovery of Scots released MacDiarmid into being himself, into being a whole (and therefore chaotic) man. And even the much praised poem "Lo! A Child is Born" seems to me trivial beside these lyrics, the language dull, its rhythms inert. Thus in that poem we have lines like:

And the atmosphere warm with that lovely heat,

but in *Sangshaw* we have a poem that relies on rhythm and language alone:

Ootside! . . . . . . Ootside!
There's dooks that try tae fly
An' bum-clocks bizzin' by,
A corn-skriech an' a cay
An' guissay i' the cray.

What is this but the sheer delight of naming, of pure creativity, as of a bird testing its wings and finding that they really work. The fact is that in his early poems in English MacDiarmid is almost less than a minor poet; we sense in them hardly a real voice at all. The leap into Scots was quite simply the leap from being a versifier into being a major poet. The difference is as awesome as that, and the laboratory is there for all to see.

Nor do we find this in MacDiarmid only but in Goodsir Smith as well, though on a lesser scale and on a more personal level. Thus it is that in a good part of *Under the Eildon Tree*, as in the poem beginning "I got her in the Black Bull," we find this fresh unmistakeable delight which the energy of the poem as revealed in the changing rhythms shows. Again it is not simply a change of subject matter with which we are concerned: it is rather as if the poet had at last found himself.

—Ah, she was a bonnie cou!
Saxteen, maybe sevinteen, nae mair,
her mither in attendance *comme il faut
pour les jeunes filles bien élevées*,
Drinkan like a bluidy whale tae.

What we sense here is not a poet writing a poem, but rather a dolphin-like joy in a new freedom, the poem being the voice of the poet in his wholeness. It is as if every individual poem springs from a central source of power which we do not in fact sense, to anything like the same extent, in Muir's verse.

And naturally also we find it, as we would expect, in Burns. When he writes in English his poetry lacks energy and inner freedom, his rhythms become dull, as for instance in the poem beginning:

> Edina! Scotia's darling seat!
> All hail ye palaces and towers.

It is difficult to believe that this is the same poet who can write,

> We twa hae paidl'd i' the burn
> Frae morning sun till dine:
> But seas between us braid hae roared
> Sin' auld lang syne,

or the quick brilliant verses of *Love and Liberty* where the doxy holds up "her greedy gab just like an aumous dish." Strangely enough, this access of energy may come from a minute injection of Scots as in the poem "Lament for James, Earl of Glencairn" which is saved by the magnificent last verse:

> The bridegroom may forget the bride
> Was made his wedded wife yestreen:
> The monarch may forget the crown
> That on his head an hour has been;
> The mother may forget the child
> That smiles sae sweetly on her knee;
> But I'll remember thee, Glencairn,
> And a' that thou hast done for me.

I think there is little doubt that when we compare the verse of the last few centuries with that of Dunbar or Henryson (I am thinking here of English verse as well as some Scottish verse) we find a diminution in ambition and in artistic complexity and energy, always excepting of course MacDiarmid and Smith. Thus when we compare Edwin Muir's "Scotland's Winter" (by no means one of his worst poems) with the opening stanzas of Henryson's "Testament of Cresseid" or the opening of Gavin Douglas's Prologue to Book VII of his translation of the *Aeneid* or even with Dunbar's "Meditatioun in Wyntir," we notice a thinness of texture and a relative lack of energy; an energy which of course we find in abundance in Dunbar's "The Tretis of the Twa Mariit Wemen and the Wedow." I would go so far as to say that what we find in the earlier poetry is the sense of a whole man speaking and that this in turn has something to do with the language itself; and I think it is no accident, though this would have to be investigated more closely, that there is also a sense of the sexual in these early poets, especially Dunbar, and Henryson in the "Cresseid," which we hardly find in Muir or in other poets writing in English, though in fact we do find, for instance in Graham and Singer, poems about women. But in a strange way the sexuality in these poets seems less natural and less rich and more accidental. Nor is there much sexuality in most of the work of the lesser poets writing in Scots in the twentieth century, apart of course from MacDiarmid and Smith; and much of what there is is sentimental as in "Tam o' the Kirk" by Violet Jacob or in Helen Cruickshank's "Shy Geordie."

There was a time when I did not sense so clearly as I think I do now this connection between language, nationhood and poetry, and one can perhaps see it more clearly in the literature of other countries which have not in fact attained complete and uncomplicated nationhood. Canada and Australia for instance, whose poetry languishes in the shadow of a greater tradition than its own and which so consistently resonates, as Muir's poetry sometimes does, with the echoes of greater masters; so that one feels that it would have been better for these countries if they had had a language of their own, different from English. What is lacking in the poetry of these two countries is in fact psychic energy, which has to do with language and nationhood, and it was, I think, a dim sense of this lack that made the recent Australian anthologist John Tranter try to import some raw barbaric energy from recent American poetry, at the expense of the entrenched Australian academics. In his introduction Tranter writes of a belief:

> that poetry was worth a serious effort of commitment. It was not seen as a pastime or a hobby: it was not a pleasant diversion from an academic routine nor a skill to be developed for its own sake. It was generally seen as an integral part of a wider struggle for freedom: freedom from conscription (we were at war with North Vietnam at the time), freedom from censorship and police harassment, freedom to experiment with drugs, to develop a sexual ethic liberated from authoritarian restraints, and freedom from the handcuffs of rhyme and the critical strictures of the university English departments.

It is interesting to see how Tranter by his use of "handcuffs" seems to think that rhyme is part of a police state. However, the energy that was derived from American poetry with its emphasis on sex and drug-taking, as if they were separated from reality, was not a true *poetic* energy; it did not reside in the language but only in statements about

Life. It was not the energy that arises from a secure language and a secure nationhood. Here for instance is a section from a poem in the anthology:

> Not life or death, just the first kicks
> of continuity. So that now,
> still surrounded by death—
> death of this, death of that,
> fly shells in the window groove,
> beetle shells among the brown leaves;
> death of these, death of those,
> 5,000 in the Phillipines earthquake,
> 3 children in an Ulster family—
> I wrote madly about life.

This is not poetry, it is journalese fuelled by an artificial energy, and not to be compared with the true sexual, yet poetic energy which one finds in the work, for instance, of Sorley MacLean.

This is not to say that language and nationhood alone can confer the energy which we associate with great poetry. We find lack of energy in much Scottish and Gaelic poetry as well as in English. What it does mean, I think, is that when great talent is present this talent has a greater chance of operating freely when it is using its own language. An alien language seems to force the poet to be on his best behaviour, to wear his best suit: it will not allow that unbuttoned freedom and free play and even vulgarity in which great work is done. What we see in MacDiarmid, as in the Burns for instance of the *Love and Liberty* sequence, is the freedom to be vulgar and sometimes obscene, in being whole, and this freedom is manifested in energy and its corollary rhythms. It is also to be found in Dunbar and ranges from the bell-like rhythms of "Timor Mortis" to the spring-like intricacies and inventions of "The Twa Mariit Wemen and the Wedow." For these poets freedom lives in immediacy at the moment when thought and feeling work together in the dance. It is at moments like these so masterfully spoken of by MacDiarmid that the language needs to be one's own beyond conscious knowledge, the power flowing into the right arm.

By condemning himself Muir was doing a brave and honest thing. There is much in his work to admire (and in fact some of his best poems are those on Scottish themes) but when we compare him with Eliot or Auden, for instance, we feel that there is a certain dullness, and that no matter how much he may try to add a cubit to his stature, he cannot write with the same freedom as they can, he does not ultimately have a language that his feelings can command. The immediacy of Auden—that casual masterful energy—could not be his, nor the rhythms of *The Waste Land*. Only MacDiarmid in *A Drunk Man* could rival these.

There seems to be a sense in which for us to be free in the depths of ourselves in the creative moment, we have to have our own language hallowed by wells of feeling, emerging freshly from one's real country. Poetry can never be deceiving, it demands the truth from us, it examines us deeply for what we are, and there is a profound sense in which we breathe along the line. Poetry is not made of words alone: the matter goes much deeper than that. The source, the ultimate energy, is in a place where language and nationhood meet, in the garden of psychic freedom where play, gravity, obscenity, are all permitted in the rhythms which are the guarantees of freedom. Poetry is not simply a personal gift. It cannot arise from the divided man. One of the differences between poetry and prose is the resonance and music of the former. Above all in Burns we sense this music, this ease of working, this freedom. And larger than that of Burns and more ambitious was the music of Dunbar and Henryson; and among these musicians, these poets whose energy is converted into resonance, are MacDiarmid and Smith and certainly, in Gaelic, MacLean.

—from *The Scottish Review* (May 1982)

Part Three

The Gaelic Poet

Modern Gaelic Poetry

A very small percentage of the Scottish population speaks Gaelic. The numbers are decreasing annually, most of the speakers now being concentrated in the Islands, especially Lewis where the bulk of the population are Gaelic speakers. Up until recently there was no television in the islands but now there is, even as far north as Lewis. Gaelic singers like Alasdair Gillies are translating pop numbers into Gaelic and singing them. We can therefore look forward to a population receiving both the message and the medium. Very few Gaelic books are published. Of the few that are published some are educational. However, in the near future a club formed in Inverness and called Club Leabhar (a Book Club) will be producing about four books a year. Some of these books will be in Gaelic, some will be in English. There is a Gaelic magazine called *Gairm* which has been in existence now for longer than any Scottish magazine of the arts. It is edited by Derick Thomson, Professor of Celtic at Glasgow University. It contains prose and poems not local or provincial but cosmopolitan in essence. There have been reviews of Pasternak, articles on Kierkegaard and the atom. It has an up-to-the-minute fashion page. The magazine of An Comunn Gaidhealach has been replaced by a fortnightly newspaper called *Sruth* which is written in both Gaelic and English and is produced in Inverness. It seems to be a sturdy child. Also there appears now and again the "Gaelic Transactions of Inverness" which contain scholarly and cultural papers dealing with sociological, historical and literary matters. Sorley MacLean and Derick Thomson contribute regularly to these.

So this is the scene. Part looks good, part looks bad. The main weakness appears to be the rare appearance of creative work, though this is being remedied. However, one must place this in context. If one compares the Highlands with Scotland as a whole, one recognises (as has been noted already) that in fact there has been at least one magazine in Gaelic (*Gairm*) which has outlived *New Saltire* and *Saltire Review* and comes out regularly every quarter and has done so for a good number of years.

Can there have emerged from such a small area, with its declining Gaelic population, against all contemporary pressures, a modern

Gaelic literature? Is it possible that such an extraordinary thing could have happened? Is it possible too that against anaemic ceilidhs, primitive breast-beating, the backward look, there should have come into existence a truly modern, a truly contemporary, Gaelic literature? The answer to this is that strangely enough such a literature has emerged. True, this literature does not have great bulk. True, it lacks any exploration in for instance the novel, but nevertheless there are in existence contemporary short stories, contemporary plays, contemporary poetry, contemporary occasional writing of various kinds.

To define the term "contemporary writing" is difficult. To know it when one sees it is fairly easy. I have been trying to define it for a number of years now. My working definition is that contemporary writing has little to do with the treatment of contemporary subjects. There are hundreds of books about contemporary subjects written in English, for instance, but these books are not contemporary. Contemporary writing has to do with the use of language, not with theme. Lowell is a contemporary not because of his subject matter but because of his use of language. So is Sorley MacLean. I would define a contemporary writer as one who charges language to its limit within a contemporary situation. This has nothing to do with subject matter. A writer can choose historical themes and still be contemporary. Shakespeare was, though in strict fact he wrote little about his own time. His sensibility, however, was contemporary.

The greatest Gaelic book of this century is Sorley MacLean's *Dàin do Eimhir* (Songs to Eimhir, Eimhir being the wife of Cuchulain). It is set in the 1930s with many references to the Spanish Civil War in which Sorley MacLean did not fight, though he often regrets that he did not. There are references to Blok, to Lenin, to Lorca, to Julian Bell, but this alone does not make the book contemporary. Its use of language does that. It can be said categorically that Sorley MacLean is our first contemporary poet of the twentieth century. The more I read him the more convinced I am that he is a major poet. Bulk alone does not make a major poet, and this is the only book of poetry that MacLean has written. Eliot's work is thin in bulk but the publication of *The Waste Land* signified the emergence of a major talent. Similarly with MacLean.

Much love poetry was written in the 1930s and this love poetry was often connected with politics. Cornford is one example who springs to mind with his verses:

> On the last mile to Huesca
> The last fence for our pride . . .

in which he remembers that "she" is always at his side. A poem like Auden's "Lay your sleeping head, my love" cannot be divorced from a political environment.

However, a lot of this poetry is vague and does not seem to be addressed to a living breathing woman. This is not so with *Dàin do Eimhir*, which is actual, historical, and true. There was this woman and MacLean was in love with her. The poetry coruscates with his love and his agony. It is existential poetry in the central meaning of the word. There has been love poetry in Gaelic; a lot of it. The greatest Gaelic love poet is William Ross and MacLean often refers to him, as in the following: "William Ross, what should we say meeting beyond death? I should mention your Oran Eile. What would you say about the poems I let loose, art-bridled, a wild cavalry for bards?"

Nevertheless, though Ross's poetry is also great I prefer MacLean's because of its vivid actuality, because of its responsibility, because of its sense of a community to which something is owed, because his poetry is on the whole not personal in the bad sense, because he recognises the break between the public and the private especially at the time of the Spanish Civil War. "Since there is no refuge and since my wish is but the empty shadow of a story there is only: Make my own spirit strong in face of suffering. For I have seen Spain lost, a sight that made my eyes salt, and an agony that put a delay on the conduct of my proud heart with nothingness and the death of heroes. . . . This, young Cornford had in his heroism, fear of the thought of his love being near him, . . ." And so on. In another poem he writes in Marxist terms (for which intellectual was not a Marxist in those days?) "Let me lop off with a knife-edge every grace which your beauty put in my poetry and make poems as bare and chill as Liebknecht's death or slavery: let me burn every branch that grew joyous above grief, and put the people's anguish in my lyric's steel."

However, not all his love poetry is political. What is startling about the whole book (the music of course cannot be sensed in translation) is the extraordinary juxtaposition of the political and the non-political, the formal and the colloquial, the learned and the simple, the tranquil and the passionate. Here is a translation of a short lyric which is Gaelic in essence and in movement. The translation is my own:

> My boat was sailing on the Clàrach
> in a benign and ocean smile.
> My right hand was on the tiller,
> my left in the winding of the sail.
>
> On the second thwart to windward
> you sat, my youthful dear,

> my swelling heart entangled
> in the ropes of your lighted hair.
>
> God if that course were steady
> to the harbour of my will
> not even the Butt of Lewis
> would appease my thirsty sail

However, not all his poems are love poems. Some are about war, some are attacks on pseudo-Gaels, some are about the dim dark way of life of the Highlands. It is fashionable to write now about the poetry of Keith Douglas who fought and wrote during the Desert campaign (and certainly his poetry is very fine), but what about this?

DEATH VALLEY

(Some Nazi or other said that the Fuehrer had restored to German manhood the "right and joy of dying in battle")

> Sitting dead in "Death Valley"
> below the Ruweisat Ridge
> a boy with his forelock down about his cheek
> and his face slate-grey;
>
> I thought of the right and the joy
> he had from his Fuehrer
> of falling in the field of slaughter
> to rise no more;
>
> of the pomp and the fame
> that he had, not alone,
> though he was the most piteous to see
> in a valley gone to seed
>
> with flies about grey corpses
> on a dun sand
> dirty yellow and full of the rubbish
> and fragments of battle.
>
> Was the boy of the band
> who abused the Jews
> and Communists, or of the greater
> band of those
>
> led, from the beginning of generations,
> unwillingly to the trial
> and mad delirium of every war
> for the sake of rulers?

> Whatever his desire or mishap,
> his innocence or malignity,
> he showed no pleasure in his death
> below the Ruweisat Ridge.
>
> (trans. Sorley MacLean)

In this poem we have the formal power and justice of the Greeks. His greatest poem in my own opinion is "Hallaig," a strange moving poem not amenable to the reason, but emerging, I believe, from a racial consciousness, uncorrupted by the strategies of the mind. This poem, like the previous one, can be found in *Honour'd Shade*, the anthology edited by Norman MacCaig in 1959. It can be seen even from translation that Sorley MacLean is a poet who must be taken very seriously indeed. He has power and emotional range, technical ability, passion, a singing quality and a consciousness of what he is doing and what the contemporary world is about. What more could one ask from a poet?

Another Gaelic poet who must be taken seriously is George Campbell Hay who is not deaf to the cry of his time, witness his "Bisearta" (Bizerta). Here is part of the poem which I think is by far and away his best: "I see during the night guard a blaze flickering, fringing the skyline over yonder, beating with its wings and scattering and dimming the stars of that airt . . . now red like a battlefield puddle, now pale like the drained whiteness of foul fear climbing and sinking, reaching and darting up and shrinking in size, growing faint for a moment and swelling like the breath of a devil in intensity. I see Evil as a pulse and a heart declining and leaping in throbs." (*trans.* George Campbell Hay). Bizerta is in flames and what is interesting about this poem is the psychological way in which Hay sees the fire. It is pale like the drained whiteness of foul fear, it swells like a breath, the breath of Evil. It is clearly as if Hay were saying that the fire is symbolic, that it is symbolic of our evil. *The fire is a human thing:* it is in fact the human heart. We made the fire: that fire is us. It is us out there.

But he has a number of other good poems too. In one set in the East he compares the vividness and generosity and spontaneity of a thief with the abstract deadness of the judge who is sentencing him. Hay decides for the thief as the truer representative of life. In this he is being extraordinarily sensitive and in fact breaking through the culture in which he was brought up. In the Highlands one of the most terrible things is to be a thief, to break the law. The Highlands are very orderly and always have been. It was remarked during the Clearances for instance that there was no violence, even though their land was being taken away from them and their homes were being burned to the ground. Hay shows therefore psychological courage in coming out for the thief against the judge and in showing himself—as the poet should do—on the side of life.

In other poems he sees the decline of Europe as the result of the war, as for instance in the following poem: "The finely hewn ramparts of Europe are down in a heap upon her plains. Their ancient carvings are spilt and scattered . . . Gone from Europe is a third of her ancient tranquil beauty . . . Och, she is become a promontory of Asia, the Balkans of the world."

It has been said that Hay has gone to school with the tight metrics of the early bards which did not allow that softening that many centuries later was to afflict Gaelic verse and lead it into a Kailyard of its own. He has some beautiful poems about Kintyre in the tradition of melodious descriptive Highland poetry, but I myself prefer those poems where he comes to grips with the reality of his time. He does not have the power and passion of MacLean: in some ways he is more tentative. His emotion (as often is the case with both Highland and Lowland Scottish poets) goes into landscape, but nevertheless at his best as in "Bizerta" he is very impressive. Like MacLean he sees that war and politics affect what we do and are. The villages, the lonely beautiful hollows, will never again be the same. Politics and what issues from them are not to be kept in a place of their own, isolated, affecting nothing outside themselves; they affect our view of the world, they destroy our world. We are political beings. Here for instance is a verse in which he shows a consciousness of this. It is called "The Hollow" (or in Gaelic, "An Lagan"): "The sound of the waves and the years between me and the praiser over there. After them, can I find in the hollow what of my soul I once left there?" It is a question which many may ask.

Hay is a poet who seems to have access to a great variety of languages. He translates from many languages including French, Modern Greek, Welsh, Arabic and Latin. One would need a fair competence in those languages to judge the quality of these translations. Some come over well, especially the ones which are like Gaelic folk poetry (as many of them are). Others, like the translations of Ronsard, are not so happy. I do not think that for instance *"gun fheòil nam thannasg"* does justice to the transparent quality of *"fantosme sans os."* But this is merely one comment on one particular poem. In general, Hay is a good craftsman with exactitude of language, disciplined and strong, but perhaps lacking in the undeviating passion of the major poet.

The third poet one must write about is Derick Thomson who is also Professor of Celtic at Glasgow University. He is younger than the other two and his poetry is different from theirs, entirely his own, and original. Where MacLean is passionate and Hay meditative, Thomson is colloquial in approach and style. His work is very Gaelic in the good sense. That is to say, it often deals with subjects which Gaelic deals with, but not in a parochial way. His work too is on the whole more sensuous than Hay's, more also a recollection of youth.

WHEN THIS FINE SNOW IS FALLING

When this fine snow is falling,
climbing quietly to the windows,
dancing on air currents,
piling itself up against walls
in lovely drifts,
while my son leaps with joy,
I see in his eyes the elation
that every winter brought to my people:
the reflection of snow in my father's eyes
and my grandfather as a boy snaring starlings.

And I see, through the window of this snowdrift
and in the glass that dancingly reflects it,
the hill-pass cutting through the generations
that lie between me on the scree
and my ancestors out on the shieling
herding milk-cows and drinking buttermilk.
I see their houses and fields reflected
on the lonely horizon
and that is part of my heritage . . .

(*trans.* Derick Thomson)

He is aware of his heritage and the division in his own mind. His first book of poems is called *The Broken Picture* (1951) and its themes are an ancestral heritage and the events of the present. History is dripping from the walls of the black houses: the old women are crouched there listening or not listening. In the sky of his own youth, however, there are planes and death. One of his finest poems is an elegy to a friend of his killed while serving in the Royal Air Force. Some are about his university days in Aberdeen. Some are about poets of the past, as "William Ross's Grave." One of the most successful is "The Well" where the theme is used to reflect the past which will never return.

His most recent book which came out this year is called *Eadar Samhradh is Foghar/Between Summer and Autumn* (1967). This I believe is a better book than the first one, with greater unity, more power, and more elaborate, purposeful image-making. It contains at least half-a-dozen first-rate poems and it is noticeable that these poems are more bitter, more savage, more directed towards the enemies who made the Highlands what they are, a beautiful but on the whole empty waste. Two of these poems I will quote here. The first one is called "The Herring Girls":

> Their laughter like a sprinkling of salt
> showered from their lips,
> brine and pickle on their tongues,
> and the stubbly short fingers that could handle fish,
> or lift a child gently, neatly,
> safely, wholesomely,
> unerringly,
> and the eyes that were deep as a calm.
>
> The topsy-turvey of history had made them
> slaves to short-arsed curers,
> here and there in the Lowlands, in England.
> Salt the reward they won
> from those thousands of barrels,
> the sea-wind sharp on their skins,
> and the burden of poverty in their kists
> and were it not for their laughter
> you might think the harp-string was broken.
>
> But there was a sprinkling of pride in their hearts,
> keeping them sound,
> and their tongues' gutting knife
> would tear a strip from the Lowlanders' mockery—
> and there was work awaiting them
> when they got home
> though they had no wealth:
> on a wild winter's night
> if that were their lot
> they would make men.
>
> (trans. Derick Thomson)

In its combination of tenderness and savagery this poem has great power.

The Clearances have haunted the imagination of the Highlanders. Neil Gunn has written about them: Ian Grimble has written a moving, ironic book called *The Trial of Patrick Sellar*. They are remarked as a turning point. It feels as if something was broken there, that some psychological irrecoverable damage was made there. Here is Thomson writing about them in his poem called "Strathnaver" (which is in Sutherland):

In that blue-black sky,
as high above us as eternity,
a star was winking at us,
answering the leaping flames of fire
in the rafters of my father's house,
this year we thatched the house with snowflakes.

And that too was the year
they hauled the old woman on to the dung-heap,
to demonstrate how knowledgeable they were in Scripture,
for the birds of the air had nests
(and the sheep had folds)
though she had no place in which to lay down her head.

O Strathnaver and Strath of Kildonan,
it is little wonder that heather should bloom on your slopes,
hiding the wounds that Patrick Sellar, and such as he, made,
just as time and time again I have seen a pious woman
who has suffered the sorrow of this world,
with the peace of God shining from her eyes.

(*trans.* Derick Thomson)

One notices the sly, unobtrusive, deadly way in which that line is slipped into the poem casually in brackets ("and the sheep had folds") and later the surge into the emotional close.

Thomson therefore must be counted among the most important Gaelic poets of this century. He has delicacy, irony, music, colloquial power, a style which is often direct but can be devious, and he hasn't allowed his sense to be destroyed by his mind.

The other poet of importance is Donald MacAulay (still in his thirties). A lecturer at one time in the Linguistics Department in Edinburgh University, he has now moved to a Readership in Celtic in Aberdeen. He seems to have been brought up (as far as English poets are concerned) on Pound and possibly on Empson. His style is completely different from anything we have been used to. One of his aims seems to be to eradicate the sometimes false music of Gaelic so that he can make statements which will not seduce the ear from their truth. In this he is very modern. All other three poets are still within the musical atmosphere of Gaelic: MacAulay seems to me to have deliberately moved out of it. He makes no concessions to the reader at all. The charge that might be made against him is that he is perhaps too intellectual, too rigorous. This charge could also be made against Gunn and Tomlinson in our day. And he reminds me of Gunn quite a lot, but especially of Empson. He has the same stern rigour, the same air of saying: "I will state what I want to state in spite of music, in spite of image, in spite of anything that will try to seduce me." Here is an example of this rigorous dry verse which still pulses with passion. It is entitled "Buying": "They ask only my sobbing in repentance for a sin that is not mine and I shall receive a freedom that I do not understand: my bedraggling in one thin wounding steeping water after another of their philosophy and gaily they would hang the washing in the heavens."

This seems to me to be a vicious attack on Calvinism, and all the more powerful because so apparently calm, so apparently balanced and judicial.

Another of his poems is called "For a Friend ":

A change has come upon your face that was like the sunshine: in the midst of your aspiring strength you received the thorn crown and knew the taste of blood on your tongue: the sod is cut from beneath your feet.

It is sad for me that today your back is towards a berry-red sun in the grey trees, that you are losing the power to hear the crackle of the frost underfoot, are moving into stillness and silence.

The words come crushed from my lips speckling the page: Guaire lives not nor Cuchuilin: O young warrior for whom are shed my tears, my mouth is not poetic.

This poem at first sight appears more emotional than is usual with him: nevertheless the use of language shows great control. And this is true even of his later poems which move more into what Gunn calls "the dark realm where we walk with everyone." These human poems are about misfits, laughed at by others, or weak for some reason either physical or psychological. Though they show concern, this concern is not allowed to become a useless pity. A mind is in charge. His first volume of poems has recently been advertised and those who have any interest in Gaelic poetry will surely buy it. In his own quiet way he is as revolutionary as MacLean, though perhaps we might wish him to open out yet more, to go beyond the "first tentative steps."

Apart from these four, who else are there? Two young poets, Norman Campbell and John Murray, are now emerging. Their poetry is iconoclastic and very funny, taking its toll of outmoded Gaelic attitudes and gestures. They seem to belong almost to a new wave of young English satirists (such as one might find in *That Was The Week That Was* or its many successors). They are exact, brilliant, irreverent and high-spirited. Their humour is not pawkish but highly sophisticated. They are subjecting personalities and language to a drastic joyful attack. In a recent poem, "Me and the Revolution," Campbell imagines a revolution which at the same time shoots down, poker-faced, snatches of ridiculous verse cruising amiably in the heavens. I like this poem for this image above all:

> and I am here on Princes St
> as happy as a bottle of Parozone.

We seem to be in a healthy period where old ridiculous verses and attitudes are being sniped at with deadly aim. Finlay Macleod in his plays seems to have partly initiated it.

Where Gaelic poetry will go from here it is difficult to say. But that it is alive is obvious. That it has a lot to its credit already in spite of the most terrible difficulties is matter for rejoicing. That there should be a Modern Gaelic literature at all is a continuing miracle. As Professor Thomson has said, it does not matter whether Gaelic will die in fifty or a hundred years. What is done even while it is dying cannot be lost if it is good enough. The medium is the message, Gaelic itself is the message. If it dies Scotland will be weakened more than it suspects, more than it will ever know.

—from *Akros* vol. 2 no. 6 (December 1967)

George Campbell Hay: Language at Large

Of the four major modern Gaelic poets—Sorley MacLean, Derick Thomson, Donald MacAulay and George Campbell Hay—the latter was the only non-native Gaelic speaker. It would, however, be very hard to find any traces of this in his poetry, since his mastery of the tradition of Gaelic verse—including its strict metrics—is complete. He is perhaps unusual in that his encounter with Arab civilisation, as a result of serving in the Second World War, made him the very fine poet he is. The richness of this encounter has been reinforced by the recent discovery of a fragment called *Mochtar is Dughall* which he wrote mainly in Italy in the latter part of the last war. And yet perhaps it is not so unusual. It was his encounter with the Spanish Civil War that made Sorley MacLean into a major poet. And of course there are many instances of fruitful encounters between civilisations, as for instance in Kipling and Forster.

Hay can be said to have begun as a nature poet, musical, delicate, lyrical and fresh as for instance in an early poem, "To a Bonny Birch Tree," with its lines:

> Sweet, sweet the chorusing, carolling and singing on the hillock when the birds of summer alight on your sprays with honey in their beaks:

or as in "Kintyre" (his adopted homeland), which is seen with affection:

> Peace from God on my fostering mother, with the incitement of love I get no rest: joy and happiness to you, Kintyre, why should I not praise a land that is faultless?
> ... Sweet is the voice of the wind on your mountains, crying on their high shoulders: lovely your white belt about you, the sea closing in on the shore.

This poem of course belongs to a strong tradition in Gaelic, to be found in Columba, and in *Ben Dorain*, to the present (and usually inferior) songs about islands by those who were born there.

This whole book, *Fuaran Sleibh* (1947), has the freshness and mastery of forms which one expects from a major poet in the making. Nor is it all of course paradisal nature poems. There are poems about storms and winds and heavy seas as in the following lines:

It was the harshness of the wind that kept me awake last night.
A wind from the south on Loch Fyne, coming fiercely with uproar

There is a poem about old age, one about the ship of life, called "Adam's Clan," which has the line, "The grievous burden of an eternal wind in her worn sails." There are one or two poems about women, and of course nationalist poems, for Hay always was a lover of Scotland as much as he was a lover of Kintyre:

> Men and women of Scotland, tempestuous race that I love, people who are not to be trampled upon, and who will not trample on others—oh, hearts that are not dull and dead, may you be a sea that will never ebb . . .

This theme of nationalism recurs constantly in his poetry, but it is not one that has created great verse: it is too exhortatory, too external, too much like poster-poetry. However, it should not be forgotten, since clearly it meant a great deal to Hay himself. Better is a poem "The Bottom of the Sea," in which there is an anti-English tone when a mother bewails the death of her son fighting for Britain. It ends, in a Scots translation:

> Sair the price maun be dounpitten
> by the island fowk for the greatness o Britain.

The more intimate parts of the poem are the most successful:

> I see your jacket on the heuk
> but the house is lown in ilka neuk . . .

(Incidentally, though Hay himself was unusual in writing in three languages, English, Gaelic and Scots, there is no question but that it is to Gaelic that he committed his true poetic imagination.)

In a poem called "Man his Own Prison?" he counsels men to be "complete and alive" like the animals. This emphasis on "aliveness" becomes more insistent in his next book. In this poem he says,

> The generous spirited heart, let it not crouch like a prisoner in a nook. Freshen the heart of the world with it. Unleash it. Be spendthrift with it. Let your back and your gaze be straight. And see the plausible

orderly dwarf people who were never but half living with the opinions of others as a march dyke around them . . .

This praise of the spendthrift, of the passionate, is of course in tune with the ideals of Gaelic poetry insofar for instance as they referred to chiefs: but of course they do not confine it to them, and in any case such praise of chiefs was in many instances an empty convention.

A poem, "The Hollow," introduces war into these fresh landscapes and Hay is to be much concerned with war in his later works:

I am today beside a far off sea under a sky whose sun never sees a lowering cloud, listening to the drumming of our gunfire, on a charmed day, warm and breathless . . .

His next book, *O Na Ceithir Airdean* (1952), is more powerful than the first one in terms of a movement from nature towards humanity. In it Hay arrives, in Keats's phraseology, into the Vale of Soul-Making. It begins, however, with another marvellous lyrical poem called "My Youth's Horizon":

Yon was my horizon in the spring and the bounds of my sight in the Maytime when the white sun of morning would return with its elbow on the knowes arising, hill upon hill in Kerry, the summits and the joyous hillsides, shoulder upon bonny shoulder . . .

But it is with the poems about Arabs and the war that Hay becomes, I think, a great poet and puts into practice the ideal of spendthrift generosity that he had already enunciated. The first of these poems is one called "Atman," a poor Arab who having had to steal from need was "condemned and reviled." Atman, unlike the judge, is a cheerful happy man, a teller of tales, a witty man with plenty of repartee:

You thieved in your need and you tried a lie to get off. They condemned you, reviled you and whipped you, and they put you under lock and key . . .

The honourable mouth that condemned you was blubberish and tiny in the grey face: and Justice was blear-eyed from scrutinising its account books and they ever showing abundance.

But the mouth which was found lying was mannerly, cheerful and melodious: I got sharp repartee and tales from it, though it was not too well acquainted with a meal.

Hay condemns the judge because he is Abstract Man, he is not truly "alive." He ends the poem by saying that Christ himself was crucified between two thieves and "it would be blasphemy, Atman, to deny that you are a brother of mine."

This contrast between the man who has lost his humanity in the service of an idea and the man who is alive in the fulness of his being is one that is at the heart of Hay's verse, as in for instance the poem called "The Knowledge that Does Not Create":

> The man of judgement and knowledge, the dumb well-informed one that does not create anything, good and bad are segregated in him in the just scales of his head.
>
> He shows with precision his recording like an instrument with delicate degrees: he is a measuring rod without any soul of growth in him: he will bring no new thing to warmth and being.

We all know who Hay is talking about here. He sets "information" over against creativity and perhaps in a world that depends so much on information we should remember that there are other forms of communication which have warmth and life. It is not simply the scientist he is talking about: it is the man who depends on measurement for a knowledge of the world: the man who has lost his soul in the service of abstraction. Perhaps this is why he writes a poem about the Prince's army crossing into England: they might have been wrong but at least they showed spendthrift passion, and that in itself may justify them.

> They closed their spell in this world with honour . . . One spell, one spell only, do we get on earth to show the temper of the metal in us, to test the edge of our courage, to win fame for our country or shame . . .

A very interesting poem is the one called "Meftah Babkum Es-Sabar?" in which he examines Arab philosophy and sets it against his own ideal. The Arab philosophy is passivity. The finger has written already and nothing can change the words.

> I remember at Suq el-Khemis while we argued in the dark café, a voice, melancholy as the voice of evening bells, that counselled me to be submissive to Providence. My own heart, your struggle against It is in vain, for every beginning and ending has been written by It already.

He gazed at the palm of his hand and went on:

> Your portion, your predestined fate and your shadow—these accompany you in every place. What is fated and has been written is a dungeon that the Divine King has locked upon us.

Hay, however, does not accept this passivity, this acceptance of what has already been set down. He opposes to it his own concept of the will:

The battlefield of our will, the hearthstone we kindle our fire upon, the field our plough-team will awaken . . .

In another poem, "The Fisherman," he sees the latter as the paradigm of the steady hearted man. "Watching and enduring are in your eye and in the gentleness of your voice."

The most powerful single poem that he ever wrote is also in this book. It is called "Bizerta" and describes the burning of that city, as seen from a distance:

I see during the night guard a blaze flickering, fringing the skyline over yonder, beating with its wings and scattering and dimming the stars of that airt.

He imagines in the eerie silence men and women dying in that fire, though he cannot hear "wailing or lamentation, the roar of rage and the yell of hate." Surely, he says, "the snarl of violence would reach from yon amber furnace the very edge of the world." But nothing is to be heard. He asks: "Who tonight is paying the old accustomed tax of common blood?"

But all he sees is the pulse and throb of the fire. "I see Evil as a pulse and a heart declining and leaping in throbs." I think this is a most marvellous image. It is as if he were saying, "The human heart created this. The human heart can be evil. It is we who created that fire. Evil is endemic in the human heart: the fire pulsates like the human heart." This clearly is one of the greatest poems to come out of the last war, in its pity, its insight, that single magnificent image:

The blaze of horror on the skyline, a ring of rose and gold at the foot of the sky.

This second book is completed by translations into Gaelic from Italian, French, Icelandic, Arabic, modern Greek, Welsh and so on.

At this point we have had no extended poem from Hay. His poetry is lyrical, philosophical, descriptive, but conforms, one supposes, to what Arnold said about the Celtic imagination, that it does not have staying power over long stretches.

The fragment *Mochtar is Dughall* might confirm Arnold's belief, in that the poem is not finished, but it certainly shows new aspects of Hay, that is, an ability to use narrative in poetry and also to get convincingly inside the world of thought of an alien civilisation, that is the Arab. Its sustained power of description can hardly have been surpassed by any Scottish poet this century. Its range of vocabulary is enormous, it is a glittering artefact with a most brilliant surface.

First of all we are told what happened to Mochtar and Dughall. Fighting in the war in Africa together they were betrayed to death by a Gefreiter. It begins:

Mochtar and Dughall, you have met in an everlasting fellowship without conversation. The walls of your gossiping house were the tortured wounded cactus.

Then, having briefly described the fate of the two men, it goes on to give a section in which Mochtar's wife bewails her husband. She asks her brothers and her uncles to avenge his death, using an image which in its tremulousness is typical of Hay in this poem: "The sweat of your hands be on his skin: the terrified trembling of his shoulders be under your palms." At the same time she accepts that Mochtar has fallen according to the decree of Fate. The savage bitter world, I suppose, reminds one of the feuds of the Highland clans, and there are many poems in Gaelic where a wife mourns for her lover and her husband.

The poem then proceeds to give the life history of Mochtar's great grandfather, who after lost battles retires into himself, becomes silent and withdrawn:

However closely the frost of his face was read, the crucifixion of his hot heart was not to be laid bare. In the Dogdays he would not move a hand to chase away the swarm of flies that buzzed about him all day.

He finally withdraws from his family and commits suicide either by default or consciously. Hay comments: "When the crystal of the heart is at its purest, how easy it is to shatter it."

But it is the next section, which deals with Mochtar's grandfather, which shows Hay at his most powerful. At this point he was writing with a marvellous ease and sense of the object. Omar is a merchant. He travels across the Sahara with his caravan of slaves and goods. He is accosted by Touaregs who relieve him of two thirds of his merchandise. His goods are described in loving detail:

Instruments of music and combs for the beard, and Korans in joyful colours, with inter-locking letters and smooth whorls which would inebriate the sight with pleasure.

Omar in his youth was the "songful, daft one," the spendthrift one, the teller of tales, "mad with the wine of youth."

The "saffron" sea of the Sahara is described with brilliance: "the unchangingness of the yellow horizon, quivering and dancing, unattainable." One can feel the intense heat of the sun, and then the coolness of the night with its many stars—"a fine golden dust dashed across the sky"—as if they were in fact emanations from the sands of the desert. This section has a quite dazzling mastery: "a magic vessel of healing was the flooding of the moon pouring down in softwaves.

It was mercy, it was enchantment, it was a dandling: it was the hand of healing after battle."

Then the caravan meets the Touaregs, "like an army of spectres, or a ghastly vision." They take from Omar most of his goods, and he and his company set off home, joyful that they have escaped with their lives. "Every ascent was a descent to us as we left them."

Omar was a teller of tales who enchanted the boy. "A long fine thread that he unwound before you, a silken thread of speech that he twined with the yellow of gold and the red of blood in it." While Omar loved life his son, Mochtar's father, thought of the world as vanity. Omar's advice to his grandson was:

> Have an open hand and heart:
> let there be courage and hardihood in you.

But his father tells him "to love humility and abandon pride. Rivers will not water the high plains." Thus in the boy there warred the "body" of his grandfather and the "soul" of his father, the joy of the one and the quietism of the other. We do not know whether Hay meant to trace in the boy the contrary advice of his ancestors, whether he wishes to show the separate world of the Scot and the Arab, or what. In the circumstances it was probably not possible for Hay to have completed the fragment but that in time of war he should have written something so intricate is little short of marvellous.

Thus Hay's journey was from nature to man and his philosophy one of hope, generosity, and courage. In spite of the vulnerable nature of his own spirit, vulnerable because so sensitive, so open to the world, he says to us, "Be alive, be human, engrave the world with your will. Do not despair." Derick Thomson, in a beautiful poem about him, ends by seeing an analogy with Ulysses, about whom Hay himself wrote a poem in his first book: "O my Ulysses—return is not your fate." And yet perhaps Hay is now entering our consciousness as a very fine poet, and one the Gaelic world can be proud of, a perfect gentle spirit tough enough to endure and make poetry of the ravages and terrors of our time.

We might end with a poem which we have referred to already and which perhaps contains his image of the poet. It is the poem "The Fisherman":

> This is how I ever recognised you, you who were brought up at the school of the fishing.
>   The man's look, the steady eyes that would search the black gullet of the storm, that would read the meaning of the sudden towering wave, as white crest showing through the blindness of the night.

Windward and leeward, watching and enduring are in your eye and in the gentleness of your voice. Kyle and open ocean, foreland after foreland with their head tides and all their winds have left their imprint on you. The swept spindrift of many a wave, calm and gale, and black tempest, have set their seal upon your cheek, man.

—from *The Scottish Review* (August, 1984)

The Modest Doctor:
The Poetry of Donald MacAulay

It must be admitted at the very beginning that the poetry of Donald MacAulay is difficult, but it should also be said that it deserves the closest scrutiny, for he has many interesting things to say, not only about the Highlands but about mankind in general. The mark of his poetry is its honesty, its care, and its exactness, for MacAulay, himself a linguist, knows perfectly well the treachery of language (and of feelings) for he writes:

> A tree was for me engendered
> by some mysterious striving:
> its branches spread through me:
> I decided it should grow undeformed
> to overcome deviant yardsticks.

At the beginning of his book *Primrose from the Stone* (*Seobhrach ás a' Chloich*, 1967) we find mostly images of despair. He speaks of those "whose face is to the dumbness": he speaks of a "cold dry wind": of a wind so powerful that "it would deafen my hearing." He speaks of the fire that he is not able to kindle because of the flood: he blows on the ashes till warmth comes. He knows very well how deep the wound of the Highlands goes, and he says,

> The warrior
> who was fair yesterday

"got lost in the dead of winter." MacAulay sets his face to this wind, and his only weapons are words that he recognises as devious and corrupted in much the same spirit as Eliot did when he wrote,

> The wounded surgeon plies the steel
> that questions the distempered part.

I am sure that, like many others of his generation, he saw the corruption that the Nazis inflicted on language and that that is why he is careful both of language and feeling. And that is why I see him as the doctor who tests the depth of the wound, putting his stethoscope to the lungs to see if there is any breath left in the patient, which is of course the culture from which he came. And that is why his poetry is so difficult, avoiding theatricals, and unearned passion, and this is why also he titles one of his poems "The Fascination of What's Difficult." There is certainly none of the drama of Yeats in his poetry, and it can be said of Yeats that there is a boastfulness in his verse which seems to have been born in the theatre, a passion for the intemperate. MacAulay's poetry could not be more different, he does not go beyond the boundaries of what he really feels, really thinks, for he has a powerful questioning mind, but one which at the same time has the modesty and decorum of the scholar.

Superficial critics might say of him that he hides behind the mind, but it can be seen on the contrary that his feelings go so deep that poetry is made almost but not quite impossible. What use, he seems to ask continually, are the expressions of feelings if they are not true feelings, as he says in the poem "A Penny for the Guy, Mister" in which he makes an attack on those who speak so glibly of "the cause"? The "question of the Highlands" is like the guy which a boy drags behind him on a board. MacAulay says:

> I do
> know this . . .
>
> that unless we have our condition
> clearly depicted in our words
> unless we have the words
> to state the meaning of our condition
> we will not apprehend it:
> we will not build a poem that concerns us.

It would be a silly doctor who would bring the correct medicine for the wrong disease: and we see this patient analysis again in a poem called "Between Kyle and Inverness," where he writes:

> for the understanding has become squint
> that does not differentiate the sincere man
> from the righteous man,
> in spite of the example.

There is a deep pain in the poetry of MacAulay but instead of flaunting his wounds like a prostitute he shuts his lips tight so that the poetry seems like the white line of agony itself. Nor is there a word in it that has not been carefully chosen and weighed in the balance.

If we wish for instance to talk of the "island home," the nostalgia of which there has been so much in Gaelic poetry (and much of it simplistic), we can find a balanced estimate in MacAulay:

>   for it is hard to state
>   without callousness
>   that the village
>   is becoming more and more narrow
>   as a world widens
>   and it is not in me
>   alone
>   that the change came
> but
>   that that state will not lessen
>   my love

And we see this balance especially in "Landmark" where he examines the whole complex of attachment to the homeland, seeing that the "question is not so simple," that that island is no longer his island, that it is like an iceberg, part concealed, part visible,

> and the part that submerged in me of it,
> sunbower and iceberg,
> sails the ocean I travel,
> a primary landmark
> dangerous, essential, demanding.

And in the same way as did Sorley MacLean, Derick Thomson and George Campbell Hay (above all the latter) he sometimes sees the island as through a foreign glass, from another land, as for instance in a poem called "Amasra, 1957," where he compares the stiff righteousness of the Arabs with that of his own island: and especially in "Navigation," where he writes of an old man who entices visitors to take a boat trip with him:

> With light step for an eighty-year-old
> his trousers rolled to the knee
> he goes out
> grabs an oar
> and stands and waits
> —an old man who in his life
> has learned good manners
> and patience
> —and who practises cunning.

(As he might in fact be an image of a certain type of Highlander). This is an eye that will not be deceived even by necessary frailty. In "Holiday" he notices how the townspeople make fun of the country people, and how the city people (those of Ankara) make fun of the townspeople, and how the foreigners, tourists, see all the inhabitants of the land as backward. This poem ends with an image warmer and more life-enhancing than is usual with MacAulay:

> under black shawls
> stirred by the wind of history
> a living eye waiting
> though burdened and disparaged:
> teeth white as lime about
> a tuneful tongue, and cheeks
> like the pomegranate.

It is not only in foreign countries that MacAulay finds his lessons but also from foreign writers such as Pasternak, who suffers the doom of the artist:

> You winnow in a country wind
> living seed out of beard and chaff
> since you have understood that those who hated you
> did not recognise
> your love . . .

and also from Gorki:

> You were engendered like an apple:
> and like a thorn you grew . . .

But this cosmopolitan consciousness does not mean that MacAulay flees to other literatures to avoid confronting the problems of his own land and we see even in that poem images of his home, as when he returns in memory to the

> path of the furrow
> of a ridge of corn and potatoes . . .

and remembers

> the first rain
> after the dryness of May

and also in the poem "The Awakening," where he writes of an

> Evening when you were a child
> playing at hide and seek
> among corn stooks . . .

Lines like these arise like springs of fresh water from the ambiguity of experience.

But MacAulay also sees the contempt that a community, even his own, can have for some of its members, in much the same way as Pasternak was despised in a large community. (In fact his critique of the community is one of the main interests of his poetry, and arises quite naturally from his refusal to be seduced by ideologies of any kind). For limits can be constricting and can lead to tyranny as can be seen in that very fine poem "Delicate Balance" where the poet shows us the destruction of a misfit in a community by mockery and derision, even though, perhaps because, his mind was larger and more refined than those of his neighbours: the man received honour only in death, which is what the community can deal with: the individual is lost in a traditional ritual.

> The day before yesterday you died;
> they let you out through the window;
> bareheaded
> they raised you on high—
> you had a place and respect at last.

It was death itself and not the dead man that they honoured in the glittering coffin that they balanced on their shoulders, a coffin which they had constructed for him in a sense while he was still alive. But it is interesting that MacAulay in the very title of the poem seems to suggest that there is a delicate balance which keeps the community alive and in being, and that a price has to be paid by the individual to maintain this equilibrium. This just scrutiny is seen again in the poem "Amasra, 1957" already mentioned, where a strict religion can be seen by another one, curiously enough, as laughable, though they are alike. One frame of reference gazes at another similar one with incomprehension:

> In the evening an old man will come riding
> on an ass,
> barefoot; sitting quite erect—
> like the righteousness of his goad—
> the strict discipline of Allah . . .
>
> In Lewis he would be a butt for mockery.

This righteousness is attacked by MacAulay in a critique of Calvinism when he writes:

> They ask of me only
> to weep repentance for a sin
> that does not concern me . . .
>
> to be drubbed in one thin
> wounding water after another
> of their philosophy—
>
> and confidently they would hang
> their washing in the heavens.

It is not easy for a mind like this, so clear-sighted, so balanced, to adhere to any ideology or to any unexamined twitterings about the "cause." Even love itself is seen with unromantic, just gaze, as when he writes:

> If only I could say
> that it was you who kept me awake
> but it was simply that sleep
> went wrong on me
> (sweetheart)
> if the truth is best . . .

(But it may not be that truth is best, in such a case, for the last line is as ambiguous as love itself may be.)

With regard to wars he sees clearly that they often arise from a clash between different kinds of righteousness:

> And the Righteous
> will issue arms to the Righteous
> commanding that the kingdom be fulfilled
> —regardless
>   of cost in desolation
>   and destruction
>   sparing not even the
>   world . . .
> Truly
> that will master
> "Sin"—
> there will be no kingdom left
> ("But the Kingdom . . .")

and again in "NATO 1960" we have that wonderful image:

> Is this
> what the end of the world will be like
> a sabbath crawling without question or frenzy?

(The eternal Lewis sabbath . . . the silence after the nuclear bomb. And "crawling" is a word that suggests a snakelike movement. Truly this mind is prolific of resemblances and analogies).

This kind of poetry is not common in any literature: this careful scrupulous voice may be easily overlooked. And yet it is a voice that is also compassionate, that has concern for the underdog. It is the voice of the doctor who cares for his patient and does not leap into the room with happy laughter and funny stories. One of the most difficult things for a poet to do is to control his imagination in the service of truth, but this is what MacAulay does, and seeks to do. He has the justice of the Greek mind, and perhaps some of its pessimism.

There is no one else in Scotland who writes at all like him, or who has this particular cast of mind, this probing, scholarly and yet fundamentally passionate clear-headedness. The forms of his poetry are modest and almost hesitant, there is no large music, no sense of big billowing sails: no, we have the sense of a poetry that searches patiently for hidden reefs, for unearned extravagances. And yet despair is not the end of the poetry, as in "Mornings," which I will quote in its entirety:

> I remember mornings
> in my first memory
> coming pale-grey from the east
> to waken me:
> early mornings
> mingling with rose-red mornings
> between memory and disorder.
> I put my clothes on proudly
> unharried by din or hardship.
>
> In the half light
> the house was astir
> with hands and thighboots
> giants paraded on its walls:
> it was warm with oaten cakes
> toasting at the fire
> scented with sea toil.
>
> If death will soon seize me
> I will stop remembering
> my shadow giants' dance
> or the dove of their kindness
> my pale rose will not be neutered
> for an up-to-date garment.

This voice is well worth attending to, for it is honest and compassionate and unconnable. It warns us to be careful both of language and of people for we will not be healed until we find the right language, the right question to ask. In a way this brings him close to someone like Wittgenstein, though at the same time he belongs in his imagery and obsession to the Highlands, and the "overwhelming question" to him really is the fate of his homeland, and the fate of Gaelic.

    —from *Gairm* (Winter 1983/84). Published originally under the title: *An Dotair Leòinte: Bàrdachd Dhòmhnaill MhicAmhlaigh*

Gaelic Master: Sorley MacLean

Sorley MacLean was born on the island of Raasay in 1911, and is a graduate in English of Edinburgh University. He was a schoolmaster in Edinburgh and later the headmaster of Plockton Secondary School in Ross-shire. One of his brothers was Calum MacLean, the noted folklorist, and another was John MacLean, for many years Rector of Oban High School.

It may be said of him that he was the first Gaelic poet to bring Gaelic poetry into the twentieth century, in more or less the same way as MacDiarmid did with Scots poetry, and for that matter Eliot with English poetry. It is true that in comparison with MacDiarmid and, to a lesser extent, with Eliot, his output has not been large and he has on the whole avoided the long poem though parts of one have been published: but in poetry quality is more important than quantity and the quality of MacLean's poetry has been consistently high. Nor has he capitalised on his growing fame by writing what might have been less satisfactory poetry than his best.

His gift has always been a lyrical one and he has thought of the highest poetry as being passionate. His own has certainly been that. He has not written the kind of intellectual poetry that MacDiarmid wrote in the latter part of his life, nor has he felt any didactic purpose. It is true, however, that his poetry has shown political concern, but political concern in a lyrical sense, that is, as politics have impinged on himself.

From the moment that his *Dàin do Eimhir* (*Songs to Eimhir*) was published by Maclellan in 1943, accompanied as it was by drawings in the Picasso style, it was clear that a major poet had emerged into the somewhat dim Gaelic sky of that time. The bulk of this book was composed of love poems which were associated with the Spanish Civil War, so that it seemed as if the love were dependent on the poet's conduct in relation to that war. It is true of course that Cornford had sensed the same connection in at least one of his lyrics, "Heart of the Heartless World": and we find the same relationship between love and war in some of Auden's poetry. But there is an extended analysis in MacLean's work which is unusual:

> would beauty and serene music put
> from me the sore frailty of this lasting cause,
> the Spanish miner leaping in the face of horror
> and his great spirit going down untroubled?
>
>   ("The Cry of Europe")

In another poem, "The Choice," the connection between successful love and war is made more explicit:

> How should I think that I would grab
> the radiant golden star,
> that I would catch and put it
> prudently in my pocket?
>
> I did not take a cross's death
> in the hard extremity of Spain
> and how then should I expect
> the one new prize of fate?

Sometimes he envies those poets who have died for the Spanish cause which he himself did not physically defend:

> Cornford and Julian Bell
> and Garcia Lorca
> it's you who have the grave
> that is hard with a comfortable glory!
> Cornford and Julian Bell
> and Garcia Lorca
> to me seven times better your death
> than the necessity of my case . . .

The range of the love poems in *Dàin do Eimhir* is very impressive, all apparently radiating from a common centre. Sometimes they are free and musical, sometimes harsh and questioning, sometimes dramatic, sometimes despairing, sometimes playful as regards language, but in all instances they are passionate, the notation of a real love affair against a historical event. And of course they are always modern. Thus for instance "The Choice" begins with the surrealistic lines:

> I walked with my reason
> out beside the sea.
> We were together but it was
> keeping a little distance from me.

He sees himself as in the same condition as William Ross and Yeats, and often refers to these two poets. In a poem which is not a love poem he also creates vivid strange surrealistic imagery. This is called "Dogs and Wolves," and begins,

> Across eternity, across its snows,
> I see my unwritten poems.
> I see the spoor of their paws dappling
> the august whiteness of the snows . . .

And yet, in spite of the newness of his imagery, he has not lost the music of Gaelic poetry, for what MacLean did above all was to fuse traditional Gaelic music with European content. Thus for instance in "The Cry of Europe" he uses the abundance of adjectives which is common in Gaelic poetry:

> Girl of the yellow heavy-yellow gold-yellow hair,
> the song of your mouth and Europe's shivering cry,
> fair, heavy-haired, spirited, beautiful girl,
> the disgrace of our day would not be bitter in your kiss.

Again, in "The Choice," much of the content has the particularity associated with traditional Gaelic love poetry:

> Is it true you heard
> that your beautiful white love
> is getting married early on Monday?

And some of the lyrics, like "Under Sail," have the free movement of traditional Gaelic poetry with their beautiful vowel sounds:

> My boat was under sail and the Clarach
> laughing against its prow,
> my left hand on the tiller
> and the other in the winding of the sheet-rope.

MacLean, of course, like many of the poets and writers of the thirties, flirted with Communism and like some of these poets he is capable of writing unsubtle "poster" verses, as for instance the following, which is called "A New Moon":

> I will put a handle on the sickle of the moon and a steel headed hammer over the feeble gold and through it: and let God call it blasphemy.
> A blood-red banner behind, emblem of hope and expectation, the standard of mankind arising, a new star lit in Heaven.

However, it is when his free and dynamic atheistic ideas, perhaps derived from Communism, are applied to his own land and to his own people that his poetry becomes genuinely powerful, as in the poem "A Highland Woman":

> Hast thou seen her, great Jew,
> who art called the One Son of God?
> Hast thou seen on Thy way the like of her
> labouring in the distant vineyard?
>
> . . .
>
> This Spring and last Spring
> and every twenty Springs from the beginning
> she has carried the cold seaweed
> for her children's food and the castle's reward.
>
> . . .
>
> And Thy gentle church has spoken
> about the lost state of her miserable soul,
> and the unremitting toil has lowered
> her body to a black peace in a grave.
>
> And her time has gone like a black sludge
> seeping through the thatch of a poor dwelling:
> the hard Black Labour was her inheritance:
> grey is her sleep tonight.

The poem in which he confronts the issue of public duty versus private pleasure most clearly is called "Prayer":

> Will I ask that my heart be purified
> from the weakness of my pure white love,
> will I ask for a flayed spirit
> even in order that I be found in the madness
> as brave as Dimitrov or as Connolly?

He feels that because of his love he is not pure enough to meet the demands of history. His prayer is in fact deception: he has evaded the issues of his time.

> This prayer is the hard and sorry prayer
> the blasphemous imperfect prayer
> the crooked perverted prayer that turns back
> the prayer that I may pray
> without praying to reach the substance . . .

Nor is he concerned exclusively with the politics of Spain, for MacLean is a Highlander with a strong pride in family and in clan. Thus for instance he writes a short poem called "The Clan MacLean":

> Not they who died
> in the hauteur of Inverkeithing
> in spite of valour and pride
> the high head of our story,
> but he who was in Glasgow
> the battle-post of the poor
> great John MacLean
> the top and hem of our story . . .

As well as this he is aware of the Irish dimension, which occurs often in his poetry in connection with its love element, as for instance by reference to Naoise and Deirdre, but also in connection with Ireland's bitter politics, as in the poem "The National Museum of Ireland":

> In these evil days
> when the old wound of Ulster is a disease
> suppurating in the heart of Europe
> and in the heart of every Gael
> who knows that he is a Gael,
> I have done nothing but see
> in the National Museum of Ireland
> the rusty red spot of blood,
> rather dirty, on the shirt
> that was once on the hero
> who is dearest to me of them all . . .
> the shirt that was on Connolly
> in the General Post Office of Ireland . . .

In fact it is evident from his acclaimed visits to Ireland that MacLean is not simply a Highland poet but a Celtic poet also.

It would be too limiting to say of him that he is only a love poet or even a political poet: there is a great deal of variety in his verse. It might also be said of him that he is one of the best war poets to have emerged from the last war, which was less prodigal of good poets than the First World War was. (One reason for the scarcity of good poets in the last war was given by C. Day Lewis when he wrote that it is no subject "for immortal verse, to defend the bad against the worse.")

A poem like "Going Westwards" brings together the love theme and the war theme, at least in the beginning:

> I go westwards in the Desert
> with my shame on my shoulders,
> that I was made a laughing-stock
> since I was as my people were.

> Love and the greater error,
> deceiving honour spoiled me
> with a film of weakness on my vision,
> squinting at mankind's extremity . . .
>
> Camus Alba is far from me
> and so is the bondage of Europe,
> far from me in the North-West
> the most beautiful grey-blue eyes . . .

Typical of his war poetry is his freedom from hatred of the enemy, whom he sees as involved like himself in a common catastrophe, as we can observe in the following verses, which contain an indigenous Highland image:

> There is no rancour in my heart
> against the hardy soldiers of the Enemy,
> but the kinship that there is among
> men in prison on a tidal rock
>
> waiting for the sea flowing
> and making cold the warm stone;
> and the coldness of life
> in the hot sun of the Desert . . .

As would be probable in a poet bred on Gaelic poetry, which proliferates with images of war and heroism (some of them, however, conventional and exaggerated), MacLean shows a great respect for physical courage—as indeed he shows for moral courage, particularly in respect to the Spanish Civil War—and he ends "Going Westwards" with the lines:

> I am of the big men of Braes,
> of the heroic Raasay MacLeods,
> of the sharp-sword Mathesons of Lochalsh;
> and the men of my name—who were braver
> when their ruinous pride was kindled?

(Yet there is little doubt in his mind that Nazism was a menace to be fought: and he does not see the war as a common capitalist conspiracy.)

A poem called "Heroes" immortalises, though not by name, the courage of an Englishman in Egypt. Physically he was not handsome, as was for instance Alasdair of Glengarry, whom MacLean refers to in the poem, but rather:

> a poor little chap with chubby cheeks
> and knees grinding each other,

> pimply unattractive face—
> garment of the bravest spirit. . . .

He was apparently not a great fighter in the "pub" but his hour was that of battle when he became a "lion . . . in the morose wounding showers." He "kept his guns to the tanks" until he was killed:

> No cross or medal was put to his
> chest or to his name or to his family;
> there were not many of his troop alive,
> and if there were their word would not be strong. . . .

MacLean ends his poem:

> I saw a great warrior of England,
> a poor manikin on whom no eye would rest;
> no Alasdair of Glen Garry;
> and he took a little weeping to my eyes.

Any essay on Sorley MacLean that neglected this dimension of physical bravery and clanship would indeed be inadequate, and it partially explains his "shame" that he did not fight in the Spanish Civil War: and the feeling that one sometimes has in his poetry, that he would, like Yeats, have wished to have been a man of action, though he did not create a sophisticated doctrine of the Mask.

Finally, one should mention his nature poetry and his poetry about his own region: and that he should write such poetry is typical, for the Gaelic tradition is full of it. We partly see this nature poetry in his symbolic references to the Cuillin, which he sees as the aspiration of man: but we find it glowing with more particularity in other poems, such as the beginning of "Dawn":

> You were dawn on the Cuillin
> and benign day on the Clarach, . . .

We see it in the movingly beautiful lines in "The Island":

> O great Island, my Island, my love,
> many a night I lay stretched
> by your side in that slumber
> when the mist of twilight swathed you.
> My love every leaflet of heather on you
> from Rudha Hunish to Loch Slapin . . .
> and even if I came in sight of Paradise,
> what price its moon without Blaven?

Most particularly of all we see it in the symphonic "The Woods of Raasay," with its quick and sombre melodies in which he transcends the straightforward descriptiveness of Duncan Bàn, for instance, with metaphors of war as in:

> Straight trunks of the pine
> > on the flexed hill-slope;
> > green heraldic helmets,
> > green unpressed sea; . . .
>
> You gave me helmets,
> > victorious helmets,
> > ecstatic helmets,
> > yellow and green;
> > bell-like helmets,
> > proud helmets,
> > sparkling helmets,
> > brown-red helmets. . . .

Again, the wood is one of "songs and ditties," as if it created its own poetry which MacLean had only to hear in order to set it down. But then as the poem proceeds the wood changes, becomes more troubled. It is not just

> The wood of Raasay,
> > my dear prattler,
> > my whispered reason,
> > my sleeping child. . . .

It becomes an image for sexual torment and movement. The adder of sex wakes in it, "the venom of the cry of pain in the love making." The Cuillin becomes a hard masculine thrust. Nature becomes a metaphor for the pains and joys of humanity.

> Poor, uncertain the base
> > on which the heroic Cuillin is based
> > just as the reason is torn
> > to put beauty on poem or melody. . . .

It is possible that this psychological analysis of the wood as sexual war is something new in Gaelic poetry. It is as if MacLean senses in the wood the ceaseless painful movement of his personal history.

It is, however, in "Hallaig" that we find MacLean's supreme poetry of his region: it is fitting to conclude with it. Sometimes in certain texts in literature we sense that the poet has reached levels of intuition that go beyond the intelligence and the reasoning mind, that he has made contact with his theme in a very direct way. I have myself sensed this often in Shakespeare and in some Greek poetry. We find it, I believe, very finely in "Hallaig." In this poem it is as if MacLean felt and sensed quite clearly the desolation, the sadness, the terrible emptiness, of the Highlands, its ghosts and presences, in an absolute intuitional music. It is one of these rare poems that have to be quoted, since the intuition can hardly be paraphrased. Here his love is

> . . . a birch, a hazel,
> a straight, slender young Rowan.

The daughters and sons of this place have been transformed into a wood. MacLean says that he will go down to Hallaig "to see the Sabbath of the dead," where all the dead people and the generations that have gone frequent: the dead have been seen alive. They are not dead at all, they are here. The girls are a wood of birches, "straight-backed with bent head." "The heartbreak of the tale" has gone, this is the immortality of all those who have lived and died in this place. Each one is again young and light-stepping. There is "a congregation of girls keeping up the endless walk." Their laughter is a mist, and their beauty is a film on his heart.

In this poem there is not only desolation, the loneliness of the Highlands, but also a deep central joy, as if there is also immortality. The poet has touched the very springs and roots of his ancestry in this most beautiful, mysterious and intriguing poem, and has laid their ghosts, since they are there and still alive.

—from *The Scottish Review* (May 1984)

Duncan Bàn MacIntyre
(written on the 250th Anniversary of his Birth)

Duncan Bàn MacIntyre, born in 1724 in Glenorchy, died in Edinburgh in 1812 and is buried in Greyfriars Churchyard. In his youth he fought at the Battle of Falkirk against Prince Charles (a comic episode in which he lost the sword of the man he was standing in for), spent thereafter many years in Coire Cheathaich and Ben Dòrain in Argyll as gamekeeper to the Earl of Breadalbane, and in his later years was a member of the Edinburgh City Guard (i.e., a policeman), a position of which he seemed very proud. He married Mairi Bhan Og, about whom he wrote some poems and whom he considered beautiful though others did not think she was exceptionally so. (But then someone thought that of Maud Gonne.)

MacIntyre seems to have been a genial, uncomplicated man and much more so than the other great eighteenth-century poet, Alexander MacDonald, who was aggressive, impulsive and a rabid supporter of Prince Charles in whose army he became an officer. His poetry lacks anger, envy and jealousy, though at times MacIntyre could make attacks on people he disliked.

It is said that his poem about the Battle of Falkirk was his first. It is a good-humoured and quite funny poem, but certainly not the work of a committed writer. As is the case with most Gaelic poets, his verse is occasional and in no sense a progressive concentration of an art scrupulously pursued. Unlike Alexander MacDonald, he could neither read nor write and he must have had a prodigious memory to retain poems such as, for instance, his "Ben Dòrain," which is very long.

A lot of his work is of inferior value. Some of it is about people of high rank and contains the usual imagery and references to impeccable looks, generosity and ability to use weapons. There is a poem which attacks the compulsory wearing of trousers instead of the tartan. There are one or two love poems which lack intensity. They are mostly to his wife and are pleasant, genial and, one would say, lacking in individuation. There is a flyting attack on a tailor who had made him angry and which has some passages:

You are a useless tough scrag: though you were in a moss hag, while dogs and ravens were rending you, they would not have their fill of food. You are often hard by the embers, your shanks to your pelvis grow mottled, and on your thighs the fire flush is intense . . .

His political sentiments are naïve. In a poem to King George III, he says that the Highlanders have proved their loyalty and are as faithful to him as "lions would be to their whelps." The king is invincible; thievery and fraud have ceased. The poor are employed, the land is rich and fertile, there are plenty of fish and much cash.

He writes a poem attacking John Wilkes whom he castigates "because he would not hear a sermon and had contempt for the church." He compares him to Judas and a toothless wolf. He calls him a cadger, a man without morals, a drunken, bankrupt, untruthful man, whose first essay in wickedness was telling lies about King George.

It is clear then that the poet was not a sophisticated political analyst, and that he was in no sense an intellectual. He lacks utterly the fierce strength of Alexander MacDonald's mind (that surrealistic darkness which for instance created the fantastic storm in the "Birlinn"), the resonance of William Ross, the incisive natural intelligence and biting wit of Rob Donn.

Why, therefore, is he remembered? Quite simply because as a nature poet he is unmatchable. It must have happened that when he was gamekeeper the circumstances for producing great nature poetry were ideal, without a shadow and without grief. Once or twice we see this happening to poets: this exact moment made MacIntyre a genius. Never again, of course, would he ever recapture that extraordinary magic, in no other place would he look and see with such apparently effortless intensity, in no other poetry of his would music and observation be so fruitfully married.

It has been maintained in a recent book on Celtic art that the Celt is quite hopeless about individualising the human form, that his asymmetric, meticulous, obsessive art is more suited to the world of nature and of animals than it is to that of human beings, that his art is fundamentally inhuman, decorative and minute. If one were to look for a classic example of this one would find it effortlessly in "Ben Dòrain." Professor Thomson has pointed out that it is really of exceptional interest that MacIntyre's best "praise poem" is not about people but about deer.

"Ben Dòrain" is based on the movement of pibroch and it may be that this variety of tempo has a great deal to do with the success of the poem, since a lot of MacIntyre's other poetry is metrically unexciting. It is interesting, too, that MacIntyre wrote a number of songs in praise of the bagpipes (one each for the years 1781, 1782, 1783, 1784, 1785 and 1789). These are conventional praise poems and are dull and unimaginative, but in one he says that "a sunbeam in the estimation of musicians in all Scotland and in London is the pipe of truest key and shape. . . ."

What one senses from the very beginning of "Ben Dòrain," however, is the authority of the man who knows his subject exactly, not in a pedantic but in an imaginative way. He knows all about the primroses, St John's wort, the tormentil flower, "the tender-spotted orchis, forked, spiked and glossy." He knows about guns: "a flint that had a cleft, a screw fixed on its head, cock that would smite it hard against the hammers." He knows about the deer, and writes of them in a peculiarly exasperated and doting manner. They are erratic, lovably foolish and changeable:

> A badger of a hind
> wallows in a pond.
> Her capricious mind
> has such vagaries.

and

> Two hundred at a count
> of the empty headed tribe
> innocently walking
> so joyously.

The deer wears "a mantle about him, attire that will not fade, a banner of waxen red he has as clothing."

The poem is utterly dependent on the music and one has to have it and the language together in any translation that one makes. Some years ago I published a translation of the whole poem (1969), of which the following is a short extract:

> The sweet harmonious hind—
> with her calf behind—
> elaborates the wind
> with her music.
>
> Palpitant bright eye
> without a squint in it,
> lash below the brow,
> guide and regulant.
>
> There's no flaw in your step,
> there's all law in your leap.
> There's no rust or sleep
> in your motion there.

> Lengthening your stride,
> intent on what's ahead,
> who of live or dead
> could outrace you?

What one gets from this poem is not only precision of detail but also a pervading feeling of love for the erratic idiots, for the landscape itself ("the finest in Europe"), a sense of warmth and harmony and sunshine.

It is interesting, however, that MacIntyre is not sentimental about the deer. He shoots them, he watches the dogs attacking them and he describes the dogs with the same detail as he describes the deer. The dog is "most ardent and impatient, venomous, yapping, nimble-mouthed at the work his kind is engaged in, with the bristles of the hair erect, so shaggy-browed, grim, sinister, with his gathered jowls wide open, he is all a-quiver at their throats." Each animal has its own nature, each is to be respected for itself.

Later MacIntyre was to return to Coire Cheathaich and find it changed for the worse. The lament for Coire Cheathaich is another fine poem. The man who has taken over is "like a stone instead of cheese." He has no feeling for either the place or the deer. "He lacks knowledge of their nature."

MacIntyre says contemptuously that he should have stayed "bent over the tub of corn husks" or "rounding up fattened poultry," feminine tasks. His gun "will not even hit the stacks." The water of Strath na Dige is like rinsings, dark and turbid, with a green pale scum on it, disgusting and foul grass-choked tarns and back-water where the water lily springs up. There is nothing else of any kind now growing in the place.

It is clear why MacIntyre is regarded as a great Gaelic poet. Nowhere else in Scottish poetry do we have a poem of such sunniness and grace and exactitude maintained for such a length, with such a wealth of varied music and teeming richness of language. The whole poem has about it the authentic feel of authoritative genius. The devoted obsession, the richly concentrated gaze, the loving scrutiny, undiverted by philosophical analysis, has created a particular world, joyously exhausting area after area as the Celtic monks exhausted page after page of the *Book of Kells*. And indeed it is that splendid word "illumination" we should be using about this poem.

—from *The Scotsman* (20 March 1974)

The Poetry of Derick Thomson

The arc of Thomson's poetry proceeds from his first book *An Dealbh Briste* (*The Broken Picture*, 1951) to *Creachadh na Clàrsaich/Plundering the Harp: Collected Poems 1940-1980* (1982). It is an arc that reveals not only more closely focused subject matter but also changing technique, a movement from the rich and sometimes "romantic" music of the first book to the barer and sparser and more ironic tone of the later books, from traditional metres to free verse.

The first book, *An Dealbh Briste*, contains many love poems. Its images are often ones of growth and decay, of doubleness, of climbing and falling. There is also the image of the rose which one associates pre-eminently with Yeats's earlier work. There is a conflict between the world of scholarship and the world of love and nature. Some of these poems belong to Aberdeen where he attended university. One of the best ones is a love poem called "Harvest Field":

> One deceptive evening, among the sheaves, with some of the corn uncut, you came by, and I put my scythe then in hiding, for fear that the edge of the blade would cut you.
>
> Our world was rounded like the harvest field, though a part was ripe and a part green, the day to work and the night to dream, and moon rose in the midst of content.
>
> I left a little to cut on the morrow, and we walked together between the swathes: you fell on a scythe that another had left, and your skin was cut, and refused healing.

As well as the many love poems (and poems about famous Gaelic poets such as William Ross and Duncan MacIntyre) there are also some which castigate the Gael for refusing to "climb" from his recumbent position. In the old days the Gael was persistent and courageous and did not stop till he reached the top of the mountain, but he now seems to have lost his courage. Thomson refers to the legend of Sisyphus with his eternal stone which always rolls back to the bottom. He takes Everest as the symbol of ambition. In a poem which describes leaving Lewis by plane he refers to Scotland and says (perhaps too hopefully in view of later events) that it "will turn its nose to the heights, / and the heart of the storm, / rising on confident wings."

There are also poems of a double culture:

> In my house, between two countries, you may see arrayed on tables, the far shells of the sea-shore and on the wall the picture of a harlot, standing at a street corner.

I think, however, that the most successful and most haunting poem in the book is "The Well" which describes in a fine image the lost culture of the Gael:

> "Nobody goes to that well now,"
> said the old woman, "as we once went
> when we were young,
> though its water is lovely and white."
> And when I looked in her eyes through the bracken
> I saw the sparkle of that water
> that makes whole every hurt
> till the hurt of the heart.

This is a young man's book, with at times rich languorous rhythms, and at times deliberately contrived, tired, repetitive ones. Already there is reference to what will be a major preoccupation of Thomson's, his loved island, Lewis, and the loss of a heritage.

The second book, *Eadar Samhradh is Foghar/Between Summer and Autumn* (1964), seems to me to show a great gain in incisiveness, power and depth of feeling, much of which is anger. In this book Thomson focuses on the enemy: it is England that deliberately destroyed his culture. We see the economic dependence on England in, for instance, "The Herring Girls":

> The topsy-turvy of history had made them
> slaves to short-arsed curers
> here and there in the Lowlands, in England.
> Salt the reward they won
> from those thousands of barrels . . .

This is one of Thomson's best poems because of its beautifully articulate imagery in, for instance, its reference to the girls' tongues as "gutting knives" by which they would gain revenge on the Lowlanders. Set against alien inhumanity is the warmth, and love, of the girls and also their fertility. The poem "Strathnaver," too, using imagery from the Bible at a key point, makes a bitter attack on people such as Patrick Sellar who carried out the Clearances in Sutherland.

Here again we find a harsh use of irony, for the Bible did not in fact protect the Highlanders:

> for the birds of the air had nests
> (and the sheep had folds)
> though she had no place in which to lay down her head.

But perhaps the best poem in a fine coherent group is "Coffins," in which Thomson remembers his grandfather who made coffins. From there he passes on to the coffin that England made for his own language and culture. He shows that even before he knew what was happening to him he was being processed towards an alien way of life and leaving his own language and his own world.

> And in the other school also,
> where the joiners of the mind were planing,
> I never noticed the coffins,
> though they were sitting all around me;
> I did not recognise the English braid,
> the Lowland varnish being applied to the wood,
> I did not read the words on the brass,
> I did not understand that my race was dying.

This is, to a great extent, Thomson's real subject, an analysis of what it means to be an "exile," to be half tied to an island and half free of it, to be half way between two worlds, to be suspended between the mind and the emotions, not to be a whole being.

However, this is not to say that there are not other beautiful poems, especially "In the Vicinity of Hol." which is a sensuous evocation of his childhood in Lewis. It proceeds like a calendar with images suited to each season, as for example this one drawn from autumn:

> . . . playing hide and seek among the stacks
> with hearts gay in the twilight, wind from the sea
> stroking their thighs and backs, raising gooseflesh . . .

(Anyone who has spent a childhood in Lewis must recognise, sometimes with pain and regret, this resonant evocation, for Thomson has the ability, rare among "intellectual" poets, of being able to recall apparently without effort the sensuous world of his boyhood, its scents, sights, sounds.)

In this book also there is a poem in praise of Lewis:

> It's your living praise I would sing
> brown little island, O island
> that wound your heath round my tongue . . .

One of the problems of reading a poet in translation, as some must do, is that one does not hear the echoes from other poems and songs which enrich his work, as for instance the allusion here to a song which speaks of Lewis as the "brown little island of the sea."

There are also sharp epigrammatic poems as when he says, writing of the coming of the electric light to Lewis, that perhaps those who receive it do not realise very clearly that they themselves are putting out the light of the language by neglect. A poem of this satiric kind is "Ribs" which brings together images of the Virgin Mary, Lord Leverhulme and the Land of the Rockets (which, of course, is South Uist, a Catholic island). In another poem Thomson says that what the Highlander needs is "cunning" in order to survive in a world of aggrandisement and corruption. A poem about Donegal refers to the sun of Ireland going down as it too loses its language, and the rise of the sun of America with "exultant clamour."

Thus it is that the analysis becomes clearer. The enemy has deliberately struck at his culture while he was unaware of it. It is an English and also an American culture that is imperialistically destroying Gaeldom.

The third book, *An Rathad Cian/The Far Road* (1970), is a series of poems mostly about Lewis which is seen as the loved one and described in sexual terms:

> How far I have fallen from you, sweetheart of my youth?
> with your brown hair and your dark eyes . . .

and

> I lost my heart to you at the start of May,
> your thighs were warm,
> firm and smooth . . .

A three-line epigram makes a point with vivid directness:

> The loom does not make the same music
> in Lewis and in Leeds:
> Lewis looms have Gaelic . . .

At this point we find not simply an attack on the English, on London, but also on Calvinism. Calvin appears in the image of the black scarecrow who enters a cèilidh-house. Folktales and card-playing immediately come to a halt. Calvin gives us "a new song." He sweeps the fire from the centre of the floor and

> set a searing bonfire in our breasts.

The fire in the centre of the floor was the traditional fire in the cèilidh-house. It has been replaced by the fire of hell. Storytelling has been dismissed as paganism. There is a great deal about religion in this books and models of ideal Gaels are set before us, such as Murdo Morrison. We are introduced to the eagle which, paid by London, anglicises Lewis:

> "My work here is done.
> I shall go to London and get fresh orders."

Different people introduced different creeds to Lewis, but Thomson looks for an indigenous creed that emerges from the island itself:

> O for an evangelist
> who would find a text on these ancient rocks.

In some of the poems there is a bitterness, an ironic contempt, very far from the romanticism of some of the poems in the first book. He refers to his island in tones of grief and hopelessness:

> When I lie down
> in your kind breast,
> the cuckoo will come,
> and wailing with it . . .

There is a simple and beautiful Gaelic poem called "The Cuckoo" but Thomson refers to the cuckoo as the bird which plunders the nest of other birds, the intruder, the imperialistic stranger.

In his poem "Though I were to go back now" he suggests that no return is possible:

> Though I were to go back now,
> though I were to step ashore
> on the eyeing quay,
> and walk the street of tongues,
> there would be no return . . .

He finds a marvellous image for his predicament. He is like a rower who in order to return to his island has to face away from it. One of the most powerful statements of his position is in the lines from "Water and Peats and Oats":

> The heart is tied to a tethering post . . .
> till it grows short,
> and the mind free.
> I bought its freedom dearly.

It is as if, in order to survive, there must be a split between the heart and the mind. The Lewis exile is not a whole being as, for instance, was Cotriona Mhòr of whom he gives a portrait. She keeps him to the "village time" with the wisdom that "flourished without books" (another split is that between books and the world of the senses, as also the world of tradition). However, the heart of the race which she represents has had a new valve put into it. The destruction of a culture is seen partly in terms of technology, the machine.

The fourth book is called *Saorsa agus an Iolaire/Freedom and the Eagle*. In this book there is much about Scotland (for Thomson sees salvation for his own culture as dependent on an independent Scotland). However, his analysis is not simplistic and chauvinistic like Hay's: it is highly complex. Thus salvation will not come by "oil." This concept only plays the enemy at his own game, since he too is materialistic. The point is, how good is the wick? One of his best poems in this connection is "Warning," which describes waiting for a birth:

> Red hand, red hand,
> the battle-cry comes nearer,
> the pain, the pain,
> the water almost breaking . . .

This is not simply the birth of a child but the birth of a nation. Thomson shows contempt for the typical Scottish parliamentary traitor by comparing him to the spider rather than to Bruce. Such a man pretends that he will save the country by exports of whisky. He would even agree to subjugate Ireland and Wales if asked as Colonel Colin Mitchell did in Aden, playing the imperialistic game. The thistle too has become bourgeois, well cared for, tidy, "the little prickles as polite as the HLI on parade" (a reference to the assimilation of the able-bodied Highlander into the army of the English "enemy"). Thomson says that he will go in search of the wild thistle which grows among the rocks. He refers to specific events such as the decision to centralise education in Stornoway which he sees as weakening the indigenous culture.

The analysis extends to the subtler ways in which the Highlander has been repressed, by appealing to his martial nature and using it against him, by inward colonisation. It says at one point:

> It is good to have a touch of the eagle in us
> though the lamb's lot is better,
> authority is good
> though it is good for the soul to submit . . .

The eagle remains an eagle, predatory, and masterful. It uses the doctrine of Christian passivity to tranquillise the natives. In another poem called "The Plough" Thomson says that before a Scottish nation can come into being there must be an end to envy, grudging, egotism, clannishness, class. Oil won't save us. We must bear our own cross on our shoulders. There are in fact quite a lot of poems about religion in this book, some of them very ironic. Thus in "Lewis in Summer" the atmosphere above Lewis is said to be so clear that God can be seen eating potatoes and herring.

> Probably there's no atmosphere in the world
> that offers so little resistance to people
> to look in at Eternity;
> there's no need for philosophy
> where you can make do with binoculars.

This, I think, is a dig at the aggrandisement of a certain Lewis religion of God for its own purposes. For instance, God is eating potatoes and herring, at one time the staple diet of the island. Heaven is naturally above Lewis.

There is also in this book "The Journey," a long poem about an alcoholic, for alcoholism is another way to evade reality. Thomson does not forget to introduce ironic witticisms:

> And if I am not mistaken
> the priest came too,
> and offered me extreme unction;
> an Irishman he was, but English-speaking;
> I heard him mention "Wafer"
> and said to him—God! What heat!—
> "Forget it, it's ice-cream I want."

Among a series of poems, *Dàin às Ùr*, not yet published as a separate book but found at the end of his *Collected Poems*, he has a caustic reference to the result of the referendum, comparing the Scotsman who didn't vote for a devolved administration to a rabbit turning back from crossing the road, after being dazzled by headlights.

> You realise
> there are sermons in rabbits
> (Scottish ones)
> this year.

Thus, one can see the journey Thomson has made. He has sensed himself at a crucial stage in the life of Gaelic. He has analysed, therefore, what it means to be a Gael in such a situation. He has diagnosed more and more deeply the disease. He is a double man, not a single man. The island itself is a double island: sometimes it almost seems like a mirage. For the language to survive, for the Highlander to survive as a real human being, there must be a way of making

Scotland into a nation. But the Scot is divisive, pusillanimous, he will not take on his own shoulders his own cross.

Oil, materialism, are not the answer. If it were as easy as that then one might as well surrrender to the materialistic forces which invade us day after day. The tone is sometimes bitter, in some of the later poems, but also healthily caustic. There has been a movement away from romanticism towards a confrontation with a life problem. Thomson, like MacAulay, belongs to those poets younger than MacLean and Hay who cannot take their language for granted, who have to leave the island in order paradoxically to see it more clearly. They have freed their minds, but at what expense. They belong to a small culture which most people do not know or care about. They are isolated as poets, yet they persist in a language which is the only one that can express their feelings. This is in no sense a nostalgic poetry. It is an unflinching gaze into the abyss. It is a study of a disappearing culture in a disappearing language. When Thomson writes a poem such as "Hol" it is not in the mood of the nostalgic poet he writes it: his detail is too exact for that. In a sense he is showing us what emotional wholeness was before the doubleness was created. It is the problem that is stated for instance in *Synge and Anglo-Irish Literature* by Daniel Corkery. Transpose Irish to Highland and the situation is the same:

> . . . The difficulty is not alone a want of mature moulds: it is rather the want of a foundation upon which to establish them. Everywhere in the mentality of the Irish people are flux and uncertainty. . . . Though not quite true, let us take it that the Irish-born child is as Irish in his instincts, in his emotions, as the English child is English: the period of education comes on: all that the English child learns buttresses, as it refines, his emotional nature. . . . How different with the Irish child! No sooner does he begin to use his intellect than what he learns begins to undermine, to weaken and to harass his emotional nature . . . his education sets up a dispute between his intellect and his emotions. . . .

I am not saying that Thomson's poetry is a handbook for understanding these things in an abstract way. On the contrary, he proves them on his pulses. It is poets like Thomson that the tourist should be reading if he wants to know about the Highlands, for the poet must tell the truth. That is his function and his fate: his "cross," as Thomson might say.

—from *The Scottish Review* (February/May 1985)

A Note on Gaelic Criticism

The first thing that must be said is that Gaelic poetry must be judged within the culture itself. There is no point in comparing Duncan Bàn MacIntyre with Wordsworth, in the same way as there is no point in comparing Shakespeare with Sophocles. Thus poets must be studied, if they are to be studied at all, inside the cultural field to which they belong.

The second thing that we must remeber is that poetry is really about language and not about ideas. If we were to say that Shakespeare is greater than Pope or Wordsworth then we would be talking about the quality of their language. We should adopt the same mode in studying Gaelic writers.

Thirdly, the problem with evaluating the Gaelic writer is that he operates within the category of the naïve, by which I mean that in general he is not an artist, his work does not echo with calculated effects. I do not mean, though, that he does not have this in the effects of language. The work of the greatest writers is not only what appears on the surface: it also has to do with the deliberate resonances that resound through the course of the work. One method of attaining this artistry is irony, a category which is not common in Gaelic literature. If this category were to be accepted as of great importance then Rob Donn would be a greater writer than most other Gaelic ones.

It is difficult to evaluate the naïve (who at one end of the spectrum is not different from someone like the novelist Alasdair Maclean). This is where our problem really lies. Lorca, though deriving much from gypsy mythology, is not himself naïve. In great stretches of his work Burns is naïve, though not in "Holy Willie's Prayer" where he is being ironical and is most an artist. Housman belongs to the category of the naïve and can be piercing in the same way. William Ross can also be moving in this sense, but his poetry is occasional. It is difficult to evaluate "Ben Dòrain" since it too belongs to this category.

The human defencelessness of William Ross is perhaps the most important thing about him. In this he contrasts with the knowledge of people that Rob Donn has, and his ability to see ironic correspondences. Though it is deployed in a small area, Rob Donn's intelligence is great. He is perhaps the most essentially modern of Gaelic writers in the centuries previous to our own. However, he must be judged within his culture. From within the culture he is, though influenced by Pope, an essentially Gaelic poet.

The catalogues of Gaelic adjectives such as we get in Duncan Bàn MacIntyre and in Alexander MacDonald were a menace to the development of good poetry, though we find them being used as late as Sorley MacLean, in *Dàin do Eimhir*.

In the same way as Burns is better seen as operating within his own culture and its perspectives, and not as a poet to be superficially compared with Wordsworth, so a Gaelic writer is to be seen as operating within his. The kind of criticism we should make of the Gaelic writer is roughly the same kind as we should make of Burns, particularly as there is a close connection between poetry and song in both cases. The problem we have with Burns is the same as we have with the Gaelic writer: how to evaluate the generally naïve, though moving, poet? As the state of Burns's criticism is unsatisfactory, so is that of Gaelic criticism.

We have to create a kind of criticism which will accommodate the naïve and occasional, and to mark it off from the other end of the spectrum which will include writers like Alasdair Maclean, and indeed most writers. Use of language and imagery must become of importance, not whether we agree with the ideas propounded. It is easy to say that Duncan Bàn MacIntyre is a great writer, but why?

If poetry in the end is a statement about being human, in language that is moving and interesting, then Rob Donn must become one of our most important poets, in many ways our most important.

Part Four

Scottish Poetry

The Feeling Intelligence

Something that has bothered me now and again about Scottish poetry—and that, of course, includes my own—I find difficult to express, except to say that it is a failure to express the immediate, and a lack of success in dealing with relations between people. It seems to me that the Scottish poets are often very good at landscape (or "nature," loosely defined) and of course, though not exclusively, landscape in winter, but that they are not so quick at plotting the quick movements of the living being. Thus when one reads anthologies of Scottish poetry one sometimes has the strange feeling that there is an invisible screen between oneself and the poem. I do not mean by this that these are bad poems, but their movement so often does not obey the movement of the living being in its odd unpredictabilities. I suppose what I mean by this is that we lack in a sense the Lawrentian intelligence whereby one senses a poem like "Kangaroo" developing not according to the laws of the poet but rather according to the laws of the animal that is being evoked.

> Her sensitive, long pure-bred face.
> Her full antipodal eyes, so dark,
> So big and quiet and remotè, having watched so many empty
>   dawns in silent Australia.
> Her little loose hands, and drooping Victorian shoulders.
> And then her great weight below the waist, her vast pale belly
> With a thin young yellow paw hanging out, and a struggle of a
>   long thin ear, like ribbon,
> Like a funny trimming to the middle of her belly, thin little
>   dangle of an immature paw, and one thin ear.
> Her belly, her big haunches
> And, in addition, the great muscular python-stretch of her tail.

This seems to me to be very pure, fine writing, of descriptive and imaginative quality, following the graph of the kangaroo in an effortless, almost animistic way. Nevertheless, moment to moment, the poet retains his control.

Now it seems to me that it is possible that this is something that the Scottish poet cannot do, and it is interesting to speculate why not.

First of all, Lawrence had the gift of taking his art absolutely seriously, in such a way that he followed it where it led him, as he follows the graph of his poem. He took the immense risk of thinking, or rather feeling, the importance of art. He lived it daringly on his pulses, as Keats advised.

On the other hand, the Scottish poet is more likely to be only half way out of his chrysalis. This is precisely what MacDiarmid was talking about in *A Drunk Man*:

> The Scottish poet maun assume
> the burden of his people's doom.

I have a feeling that in that sense the statement would have been meaningless to Lawrence. It is true that no artist has freed himself from the pull of his time and its preconceptions, but MacDiarmid is talking of something different. He is saying throughout the poem that no Scottish poet will ever be whole, that he must always be the twisted thistle, preoccupied by the wrestle between the soul and the body, between mind and the deadness of the material around him.

Furthermore MacDiarmid eventually took the way of scholarship, which is always the danger for the Scottish poet. He took the direction of philology and ideas, as in *In Memoriam James Joyce*, because in a sense he did not trust art enough. In many of his early lyrics he did have this Lawrentian femininity, but he distrusted it, it was not saying enough. And therefore it was trivial.

It is as if Scottish poets are trapped into logic and the disciplines of the mind, as for instance W. S. Graham in a long poem like "The Nightfishing" where a slightly crazed metaphysics takes over from simple description. Burns Singer was another destroyed in the same way.

Thus it is that the Scottish poet never quite trusts the trembling delicacies of the poem unless it is saying something logical, something that can be paraphrased. And often something moral: that is to say, unless the subject matter of the poem can be categorised.

This is true of as early a poem as Henryson's *The Testament of Cresseid*, though his portrait of Cressida is unforgettable and true. Nevertheless the ultimate difference between himself and Chaucer is that Chaucer allows his people to be what they are without moralising about them. He allows the fecundity of their being, and for him in art there are no terms like good and evil. His intelligence is such that he leaves the reader to make deductions. What would the Scottish poet have made of the Friar and the Monk? How heavily he would have cast his net of morality over them! Nor is this the case with Chaucer only. What a difference there is between Dryden's *Antony and Cleopatra* and Shakespeare's. And of course when we speak of Shakespeare we are speaking of the ultimate writer in this plotting of the living graph.

I take it that this is precisely what preoccupied Robert Lowell. At the beginning of his career he wrote a sort of willed poetry choked with detail, still enmeshed in the New England atmosphere, and his problem was to break from that into a freer poetry. However, I do not think he ever achieved the Lawrentian quickness and mercurial chameleon lightness, but he did eventually break his chain mail to emerge at least into the simplicities of *Day by Day*. Here the moralist had been abandoned and the poems became the notebook. One feels, however, that such lightness is not in tune with the habits of his mind.

We do not find this lightness only in the poems about animals by Lawrence. It is also true of the people in his novels, particularly the early ones, in which the prose allows them to breathe. Is this true of Scottish novels? On the contrary, many of them show the influence of direct morality or its reverse side. If the characters are not the fairy tale ones of the kailyard they are often the opposite, that is to say the grim characters of a book such as *The House with the Green Shutters* by George Douglas Brown. How many of them actually breathe along the nerve, as for instance they do in Tolstoy? How many of them do not live in an eternal sunniness or an eternal grimness? There is an exaggeration in one direction or the other so that we do not often see these characters as they are in their full and unpredictable roundness. Thus we often see in the Scottish novel that the characters exist in an idea which they illuminate more or less crudely.

We find this immediacy which follows the movement of the human feeling in a poem like "Asphodel, That Greeny Flower" by William Carlos Williams. Sometimes (naturally) other things that we expect from poetry have to be sacrificed in order to get at the living nerve, the movement of the feelings, such things as an absolute precision of language. This, however, is a risk that is worthwhile taking, sometimes; and we are not in fact arguing that this kind of poetry is the greatest poetry, we are only arguing that it is a kind of poetry that is almost closed to the Scottish poet.

It is a spectacle of the utmost sadness to see MacDiarmid, an indisputably great poet and one who sometimes took the risks of the immediate—though often in political matters—become at the end the lonely poet who scrutinises stones as if he were living in the middle of a desert among people whom he could not reach; one who turned away from the ordinariness and the miraculous spontaneities of living because he could not trust his feelings enough. And it is a lesson to us to see Williams—an infinitely lesser mind, I think—following so apparently carelessly the graph of his own feelings.

What I suppose it comes down to is this, a kind of defenceless openness, a willingness to say that the world is good in spite of. . . . But the question is how can a poet in Scotland retain this defenceless openness? In order to survive he has to build a shield around himself and this shield becomes more amd more himself. It is true that the idiot is the true poet in Dostoevsky's sense but how be the "idiot" in Scotland? For there is a tradition of the village idiot already. And how remain true in the unrelenting earnestness of the life of the intellect in Scotland? And how retain the sense of art as play, which does not have to do with good and evil?

The intelligence in Scotland has been *par excellence* the intelligence of the practical. We could enumerate endlessly the practical inventiveness of the country's scientists and engineers. But this has been at a cost, and the cost has been that it has disguised and rendered void the vision of that other kind of intelligence which Lawrence shows. Thus in Scotland there has been on the one hand the cult of poetry as "inspiration," an absence of the intelligence; and on the other hand the cult of the intelligence as aggressive and logical. MacDiarmid reacted against the former but tended towards the latter. What he missed in his later poems was that other sort of intelligence which his own lyrics show, the self-delighting intelligence of the feelings. For we are not to say that these lyrics are divorced from the intelligence and are simply inspiration. On the contrary, they are wrought with the fiercest intelligence, as are Blake's lyrics. They are not untutored, or inspirational. Neither, of course, are the poems of Lawrence.

Thus it is that we say that this sort of poetry is not necessarily the greatest poetry but it is a category in which Scottish poetry is weak. It is possible that if we were to search out how our great scientists made their discoveries, we might find that even they had made them in a Lawrentian manner, that is to say, by feeling and intuition. But our Scottish education does not work like that. It must explain everything, as in the questions and answers of the Shorter Catechism. It will not allow the intelligence to be other than that of the relentless logician. Everything must be explained, and nothing is explained, And that is possibly why in our Scottish schools there has been such a terrible failure with the children, with their intuitions, their unpredictabilities. It is because the feelings have been lost, it is because we are afraid of our feelings, and we have substituted a dead intelligence in their place.

It is for the Lawrentian intelligence that we should be seeking, the intelligence that is omnivorous of life itself, of its ultimately uncategorisable movements. And our failure in this can be shown by our stubborn failure to show adult emotions, their to-and-fro tides of jealousy, possessiveness, love, delight, which the great Russians are able to do because they almost seem to come to novel writing without any preconceptions except the respect for life. In this sense some of MacDiarmid's later poems compose a great mortuary document of the Scottish psyche noting down with crazed scholarship its contradictions, its remorseless devouring mind. After *A Drunk Man*, MacDiarmid leaves the way of the living intelligence, and adopts the way of category. Yet who would choose the way of category for:

> O whaur's the bride that cairries the bunch
> o' thistles blinterin white?
> Her cuckold bridegroom little dreids
> what he sall ken this nicht.

For the poet in Scotland there awaits logic, scholarship, metaphysics, but there also awaits, if he has the patience of the feeling intelligence, the living quick of life itself. Perhaps he should choose the latter more in the future, if his tangled languages, his education, his claustrophobia, will allow him.

Sea Talk by George Bruce

Poetry does many things. One of the things that it does is to establish in one's mind an area, a region. George Mackay Brown does this for Orkney, George Bruce does this for the North-East of Scotland. Because of his Catholic beliefs, Mackay Brown's Orkney appears aureate as well as Norse, colourful as well as sparse. The virtue of Bruce's poetry as shown in *Sea Talk* (1944) is that he allows the North-East to speak for itself in a harsh clipped speech. For those who have lived in the North-East of Scotland, Bruce's poetry establishes it forever. He has found for it the exact speech, the exact notation. It is in fact the poetry of a region that does not believe in poetry. For this reason the poetry is bitten off on the tongue as if it were embarrassed to be poetry. It is poetry that is close to prose and yet it is not prose because the poet feels deeply in his bones what he is writing, so deeply that poetry is the only fit instrument for his feelings, as in "Inheritance":

> That which I write now
> Was written years ago
> Before my birth
> In the features of my father.
>
> It was stamped
> In the rock formations
> West of my hometown.
> Not I write,
>
> But, perhaps William Bruce,
> Cooper.
> Perhaps here his hand
> Well articled in his trade . . .

or as "In My House":

> My house
> Is granite
> It fronts
> North,

> Where the Firth flows,
> East the sea.
> My room
> Holds the first
>
> Blow from the North,
> The first from East
> Salt upon
> The pane.

One might conceivably argue that these are notes for poems rather than complete poems, but one would be wrong. These poems are not notes in the sense that other poems might have come from them. These are the poems themselves and they stand up solid on the page, as solid as the people who would find it embarrassing to write poems or speak in a large way. Thus these are poems because any aureate language is avoided by a people who do not believe in aureate language, for whom in their struggle with their elements an aureate language would be superfluous and false.

> Halfway up the stairs
> Is the tall curtain.
> We noticed it there
> After the unfinished tale.
>
> My father came home,
> His clothes sea-wet,
> His breath cold.
> He said a boat had gone.
>
> He held a lantern.
> The mist moved in,
> Rested on the stone step
> And hung above the floor.
>   —"The Curtain"

This is one of the most difficult kinds of poetry to write for the reason that the poet is trying to keep himself out of the poem. He is inexhaustibly restraining himself to use a language that would be a betrayal of the facts. Sometimes Bruce does not avoid this temptation and then he fails as, for instance, in "Boys Among Rock Pools": "They hunt (O primitives!) for small fish." The "O primitives!" is wrong and feels wrong because Bruce is speaking and looking down on the boys. It is difficult for a poet not to do this, not to look at his creations as if from above, but most of the time, miraculously, Bruce does not do this.

Bruce is in fact trying to do one of the most difficult things it is possible to do. When one considers, for example, the poetry of Shakespeare one realises that what Shakespeare is doing is using all the resources of language. It is possible that the characters in Shakespeare's plays and poetry would use all linguistic resources since, in many instances, they are highly self conscious beings. On the other hand when one is writing about beings that are not highly self conscious what does one do? It is possible that one will do as a Synge does and imagine that his peasants will speak creatively and imaginatively, and perhaps they do. Bruce's people are not Irish, they are not linguistically exuberant, they do not love poetry. Nevertheless this does not mean that they do not live and have experiences. Thus the poet is faced with the problem of finding a language for them. The language he finds for them must represent them. And the language that Bruce finds for them involves him in forgetting much that he knows as a poet: he is writing, as he himself says, about a "land without myth," a land without resonance. But in one of the paradoxes of poetry the language without resonance acquires its own resonance. And it acquires resonance the more the poet does without "poetic" resonance. Thus when the poet writes using the resources of language he fails, as in "Sea Talk":

> Consider the spider crab.
> From the rock, half rock itself, pinhead eyes project,
> The mechanism of movement awkward, legs propelled
> A settlement for parasite, for limpet;
> Passionless stone in the world of motion.

This is too self-conscious and reminds one of Auden. But, on the other hand, when the poet withdraws to make room for his people, he writes ("A Boy's Saturday Night"):

> In summer the sky
> Was lit late.
> Nearby the beach
> Were stalls, swing boats.
>
> Steam-driven round-abouts
> Gold horses of wood
> Or bright red chair-o-planes
> And mechanical music . . .
>
> On the links stood
> A boxing booth.
> "Boys half price for the boxing."
> The fishermen spent money here.

One would again think that these are notes for a poem and one would be wrong. For the words emerge from that world without drawing attention to themselves. They are, as it were, emanations from that world, they exist in it as organisms. They themselves live in that world, they are like the crabs of which Bruce writes. The poet has no place in that world, he is not really celebrating it, he is letting it speak. In that world the poet of aureate language would look ridiculous, he would only draw attention to himself. Thus the poems must not look like poems. The price of their being written is that the poet must appear to forget the ornaments of art and must learn that most difficult of arts, which is to write as if there was no art involved.

> The crab scuttles on the sea floor.
> Hook dangles, net opens to the tide.
> The boat's keel is still or moves
> With the greater water movement.
> Between the thumb and the first finger
> The weighted line.
> —"A Land Without Myth"

One would almost think that anybody could write that, as if it were not poetry at all. It is such spare poetry that someone might say, "Who does he think he is? I could write this myself." The trouble is the person who said that would not be able to write it. For in the end it really does not matter who writes it: for the poet is not interested in self glorification. He is only interested in fixing his people, his place, in letting them speak through him:

> As he comes from one of those small houses
> Set within the curve of the low cliff
> For a moment he pauses
> Foot on step at the low lintel
> Before fronting wind and sun.
> He carries out from within something of the dark
> Concealed by heavy curtain,
> Or held within the ship under hatches.
> —"The Fisherman"

I think that all these poems gather to one particular poem—"Kinnaird Head"—which is objective and beautiful. He has not quite succeeded, and yet he has almost succeeded. He has risked a greater richness than the region demands and he has put himself at the centre. In one way (I am thinking of the last four lines) he has, I think, failed but in another way he has succeeded. The reason why I think he has succeeded is that in spite of the last four lines he has written a poem about the area in a way that reveals it in an exact and singular way. There is a point where the poet has to bring to bear the resources and music of poetry if he is to write about his area. Even William Carlos Williams has to do that in "Paterson." The difficult point is this: how is one to make that kind of sparse music which reflects the sparse mind of the area? Any failure in the poem is in fact a necessary failure. It is the impatience of the poet who finally feels that it is necessary to eke out the resources of his speechless, perhaps dour, people.

KINNAIRD HEAD

I go North to cold, to home, to Kinnaird,
Fit monument for our time.

This is the outermost edge of Buchan.
Inland the sea birds range.
The tree's leaf has salt upon it.
The tree turns to the low stone wall.
And here a promontory rises towards Norway.
Irregular to the top of thin grey grass
Where the spindrift in storm lays its beads.
The water plugs in the cliff sides,
The gull cries from the clouds
This is the consummation of the plain.

O impregnable and very ancient rock
Rejecting the violence of water,
Ignoring its accumulations and strategy,
You yield to history nothing.

Towards the Human:
The Poetry of Stewart Conn

There are many poets whose first books are their best and whose next books represent a diminution of freshness or complexity. Stewart Conn does not belong among these, for the interesting thing about his work is that it has got better and more individual the more he has progressed. It is a hard struggle—as it must be in our time especially—to eliminate from one's work the voices and echoes of others, to become more progressively oneself, to listen to what oneself has to say without bravado, without immodesty.

Thus his first book, *Thunder in the Air* (Akros, 1967), is not one of Conn's best. I sense in this early pamphlet the influence of Norman MacCaig on the one hand and on the other hand a conscious literariness which is often the enemy of the poem. Thus for instance "Summer Farm" has lines like:

> Pitchforks
> Flash and fall. Bales are fiery ingots.
> Straws sputter like squibs. . . .

And in another poem, the title poem of the collection, we find the lines:

> Cows slump in pastures, crop
> Pale clover, are yapped at
> By threadbare dogs. . . .

This seems to me to be MacCaig country, though certainly Conn does not in these poems philosophise in the way MacCaig sometimes does, but contents himself with description. However, the statements appear to be there only for their own sake as if a theme weren't as yet present, and this probably accounts for their staccato nature. The world is simply a set of images and metaphors hardly related to each other.

True, beyond image-making accomplishment there are hints of a more serious engagement as yet only glanced at in a desultory manner. Thus the best of the literary poems is "A Student of Russian Literature" in which the protagonist finds a diminishment of self in literature so that in the end he will die "literate—but having ventured little." It is almost as if Conn had realised a possible danger for himself.

On the evidence of this first book one would have to say that Conn is a poet who plays with images very often of a sparkling nature, sometimes in an exaggerated manner—"stones explode"—but who nevertheless shows great care for language, some evidence of being interested in people—people he has read about as much as people he has known—but that in some way his verse is not yet deeply committed enough because he has not yet found a theme. Technically he is very well equipped, achieving easy effects without much apparent effort. And we might advise him, "Trust yourself. The world is not an aesthetic model. Try and work more against the grain instead of with it."

His second volume, *Stoats in the Sunlight* (published a year later by Hutchinson), shows greater maturity but has some of the weaknesses of the first book. As before, literary references are liable to mar a poem like "The Orchard" where a series of formalised images—again aesthetic and slightly remote—includes one about pigs who are said to be "crude as Caliban." The images are as bright as ever and the writing exact, though sometimes one feels that it is not quite Conn's own. There are poems about Troy, about Renaissance Thought (the colour and life of the Renaissance and Elizabethan England have a great attraction for Conn), about knights, about Rilke, about Rimbaud. There is a poem called "Ambush" which is of the same kind as "Victim" and "Flight" in the first book. This poem, however, picks up the title image of the book at the end in a splendid, decisive, though rather distanced image:

> The next day it was spring. Trees were traced
> against an elegant sky. Without getting up
> I tried to remember the dream. I found
> my hands still tied. And there,
> stripped and dripping like stoats in the sunlight
> were eight men fastened through the throat to trees.

As in the first book the movement of the poems is adroit and easy. Conn does not usually allow emphasis to lie on the rhymes where there are any but will end his sentences in the middle of a line, thus giving the poem a conversational effect.

He has not yet worked through his influences, however, nor his habit of making images for their own sake, nor his enchanted gaze at the "beautiful." Nevertheless there are a number of poems which suggest that he is becoming more and more confident, more and more immersed in what he is saying. For instance "Rat Catcher" for most of its course is a fine poem only spoilt by the too glib reference to Hamelin. But there are beautiful liquid sentences in the poem, as for instance the second stanza:

> He lets them swarm, then wets his knife
> along their throats. Shiny with sweat
> he fastens on. Immortal catcher
> he snaps the bones under their feet.

There is some lovely but not "beautiful" writing in "The Clearing," as in the opening lines:

> Woodsmoke, sheer grape-bloom, smears
> The trunks of trees, flecks larches
> Lilac and as deftly clears.
> Startlingly among patches
> Of sunlight, come glints
> Of steel: the workmen are at it
> Early. Bright-jerkined, gigantic
> In quirk lightning they flit
> Under branches, making markings,
> Or, smirched, become blurs
> Of themselves. . . .

This is very fine dense writing with some lovely touches, as for instance the use of the word "tricks" and the sense of dapple created by the intricacy and movement of the language, not in a painterly manner but in a truly poetic one. It is easy to see why this is so different from early "beautiful" writing: it has to do with a deeper commitment to the material, to the lengthening of the sentences, to the more loving attention that is paid to the subject matter and not to an ornamental style.

But the question remains. Where is he going to go? Is he going to go like Hughes towards the world of the animals or landscape, or is he going to concern himself with people? There is evidence of course that both directions are possible, for among the poems in both books are ones that deal with tyranny and oppression of some kind or another—a few anonymous in their locality but one at least precisely placed—and there are many poems that deal with animals such as horses or ferrets or stoats or rats. One would be inclined at this stage to think of Conn as a poet whose main danger will be his love of the "beautiful" and the ornamental but from whose work along with images of violence there rises now and again a concern for the victim and the socially repressed. Would his own path through life abolish the literariness from his work or not?

Conn's next book, published by Hutchinson in 1972 and called *An Ear to the Ground*, answered the question very decisively. In this book there is a clear dramatic leap forward, and this leap is in the direction of human concern. Gone are the animals: gone for the most part are the aesthetic poems: and instead we have poems about people in the midst of their mortality. Conn is writing from within "the world of all of us."

A poem which echoes part of the title shows what is happening. It is as if Conn had heard in his own life the sounds of approaching dereliction and death, threat and pain. The poem is called "Tremors" and in it Conn recounts how he and others used to put their ears to the rail to hear the sounds of approaching trains, and this simple yet profound image generates a resonance out of all proportion to its simplicity. In those days, he says, it was a childish game but now it is a "matter of survival."

> It is more and more
> A question of living
> With an ear to the ground:
> The tremors, when they come,
> Are that much greater—

This sense of urgency is echoed in another poem called "Message from an Island." He imagines himself on an island with air so rarified that he has no shape. He cannot "thrive on the vocabulary of isolation." He must return to the mainland with its "proven means of communication." He scans the horizon as he seals a message in a bottle while:

> The sun
> Is a red flare, a crate of oranges smashed
> By the green Atlantic.

Images come to him of the remains of women and children lashed together and thrown into the Mekong. It is no longer aesthetic Elizabethans with their swords that he sees but real possible killers in our own world. The poem ends:

> Meanwhile
> The darkness gathers and swivels
> Towards me, the barrel of a great gun.

In a poem called "Lilypond" he watches decay and change. Years ago the water was clear.

> Now its spars
> Are smashed, the iron flamingoes
> Gone. . . .

But he will not be there when the area is filled in and the pond is drained. This leads him to remark:

> In so many ways we avoid
> Being in at the death;
> Preferring to let nature take its course.
> And putting in an appearance
>
> When we know all is safe.

"Journeying North" is a fine poem which picks up the train image again. Conn is heading north towards Scotland after having seen at the Tate a Magritte exhibition which includes, among other paintings, a portrait of a couple kissing each other through sacking, another of two Edwardian figures attacking each other with club and net, and yet another of a nude with blood pouring from her mouth. The poem ends:

> The air thick with tobacco smoke,
> We near Gretna. Heavy anvils strike.

It might at first sight seem as if this poem belongs with those earlier "aesthetic" ones. In a certain sense this is the case since it is generated by works of art. But in another truer sense this is not the case. For whereas in these earlier poems Conn was articulating an ornamental style, here there is a real feeling of an external menace and the poet clearly conveys the threat to his wife:

> Imagine you laying my meal
> On a frail cloth that might
> Have been a bridal veil. . . .

There is also a number of poems which have to do with his father, one in which he sees him taking hours to lay linoleum when at one time he used to be so dapper. He takes his mother through the Botanic Gardens where the bandstand is now gone with the great rain barrels that used to be there.

> Everything is now neat and plastic.

Poems about his wife show an unwavering concern for marriage.

It is clear what direction he has taken. He has left behind him admiration for the violent and the colourful. He has found himself in a world of sickness and frailty, of dying and death. And his language and rhythms beautifully accommodate themselves to that world. His style has become an effortless instrument for recording and he has a new ability to move the reader. Where he is literary now he is so with a real purpose, as for example in his poem "Summer Afternoon" where the two italicised lines

> *Shall we, nearing extremity,*
> *Be equal objects of distaste and pity?*

reinforce and give greater weight to the statements made in the poem.

Conn's recent collection *Under the Ice* completes a quartet of ominous titles, *Thunder in the Air, Stoats in the Sunlight* and *An Ear to the Ground* (water, air, fire and earth). The tremors out there are coming closer with each book. This latest volume has, I think, less glitter than the other books and is more wintry in its atmosphere. It focuses more clearly on the domestic world of the poet and his family and sees them as beleaguered in a dangerous environment. It is in essence a book of love poems, tender and clear-eyed, for what distinguishes Conn's writing at its best is his capacity for feeling, for the fine delicate mesh of our diurnal lives.

We are balanced like Raeburn's confident though slightly comic parson on thin ice. But whereas the parson gazes straight ahead, we look down. In a poem called "Visiting Hour," Conn begins obliquely by describing goldfish under ice ("five orange stains") which are rescued by the breaking of the ice with a hammer. The poem ends:

> That it should come to this.
> Unable to hide the horror
> in my eyes, I stand helpless
> by your bedside and can do no more
> than wish it were simply a matter
> of smashing the ice and giving you air.

A poem called "Bonfire" describes the difficulty of being neighbours. Conn has quarrelled with the people next door because the oldest boy has broken one of his wife's favourite shrubs. He is lighting a bonfire and suddenly realises, as every twenty minutes a different gentleman comes from next door and girl follows girl, what he is next door to, though his is a "respectable neighbourhood." The bonfire itself becomes an image of his sudden desire, mixed with nausea, and the whole poem a metaphor of our wish to defend our own territory and our family while at the same time we yearn for the menacing and the disordered.

A poem called "Arrivals" tells of his waiting for his wife at an aerodrome behind "plate glass."

> I watch
> with a mixture
> of longing and despair
> as you re-enter
> the real world.
>
> All we have is each other.
> I sometimes wonder
> if that is enough;
> whether being together
> enlarges or diminishes grief.

Ice, plate glass: both represent the distance between people, as also does the spun glass of the moon explorer's helmet, or for that matter, the window of a car wound down in the Bear Park he is visiting with his wife and child:

> Looking sideways at you
> I wonder how often I wind
> Equivalent windows blindly down . . .

Thus below the ice there beat and thresh terrifying energies such as that of the killer whale who "charges the ice with his forehead." The poet hears his wife moaning in her sleep and knows that she is far out on her own:

> Seeing as though through ice
> Blurred forms gyrate, we will put our heads
> together and try to batter a way out.

Conn, in this impressive collection, has learned to speak with a quieter, soberer voice, denying himself the glitter of his early poetry. Without surrendering to the easy emotionalism of the confessional poet, he has found a way of teasing poems out of the daily routine, quiet, gentle but wise and echoing poems. The power of his writing can be shown by this poem from the book called "Reawakening" with which I will conclude:

> "Worse than that, the walls smeared
> With excrement: adults with the minds
> Of children, behaving like pigs
> At a trough; men circling the yard,
> Each with a hand on the shoulder
> Of the man in front. One patient
> Kept in a padded cell, lest he rape
> Someone as he did his mother
> In '24: the face frozen, body slow
> But for the hands' constant fever."

My father has not broached the subject
Of his thesis, *encephalitis lethargica*,
For as long as I can remember. Today
I showed him an article in *The Listener*
Describing how a new drug had awakened
A group of patients in America: one woman
Paralysed forty years leapt to her feet,
Ran round the ward, shattered inmate
And doctor alike—then had to face
Being two ages, at the same time.

"Most frightening, the moral decay:
One female student caught the disease
(This confirming its infectious nature)
And soon had the University in a turmoil.
How she ended up, I couldn't say . . .
Thanks for underlining these sections . . .
That helps . . . The strongest argument I've known
For euthanasia: the wrong side
Of the story of the Sleeping Beauty,
No cure known, least of all a kiss."

Putting the paper aside, he tells
Of the research he did: using expressions
He must have thought he'd forgotten:
Referring to a thesis that has lain
In a drawer for forty years:
His mind awakening, at the one time,
To what he did—and what he might have done.

  —from *New Edinburgh Review* (Summer 1983)

The Power of Craftsmanship

Robert Garioch's poetry does not have the intellectual adventurousness of MacDiarmid's nor the glamour and sensuousness of Goodsir Smith's, and yet it seems to me to have a quality which neither of these had to the same extent, that is, accessibility to the consciousness of the ordinary reader. It has a peculiar honesty of its own, a vulnerability and openness that is very attractive. It might very well be that we would turn to this poetry when the lights are low, when we suffer from boredom, from being, as he himself would say, "scunnert." And we would turn to it sometimes for relief in laughter since Garioch is by any standards a very funny poet, not only funny in what he says but in the detail of his craftsmanship (the rhymes that he finds, time and time again, in his sonnets are quite outrageously funny and ingenious). He can be funny in the way that "Embro To The Ploy" is funny, that is in a sunny, cheerful, uncomplicated way: or he can be funny in an unexpected way as when for instance he compares heaven to

> Badenoch in simmer wi nae clegs about:

or he can be funny in the sudden seizure of paradoxes (for this is a poet with a very sharp eye) as, for instance, in "Two Festival Sketches," or in the equally sudden illumination of images as in "Queer Ongauns":

> ... a beadle of some sort displayin
> frae ilk front sait a muckle siller cosh:

or in the sublimely beautiful ("Festival 1962")

> some pacing provost—Thon yin's Aronowitz—
> passes, to music frae *Die Meistersinger*,

or he can be funny as when with a final nail he closes the coffin of the sonnet "Elegy" with the words,

> Weill, gin they arena deid, it's time they were.

In fact much of his wit depends to a great extent on his mastery of craft; it arises almost as a solution to a technical problem. In general he is not hugely creative of imagination, but can write the most serenely beautiful lines.

One sees him as the perpetual observer, the small man on the edge of things watching closely the doings of the great, and this whether he is translating from Belli or walking through his own Edinburgh. His Edinburgh is not the highly resonant one of Goodsir Smith, not a theatre, usually nocturnal, for love stories and glamour. This Chaplinesque figure always appears in the daytime watching the officials' Rolls Royces, worms sliding out of cracks in pavements, poor people as well as rich. Garioch is too intelligent not to see he cannot abstract himself from the hypocrisies around him, and his admission of his own weaknesses is a great deal of what endears him to us. But by choosing to translate Belli he has distanced himself from his material and can comment on it freely and almost impersonally. Belli is his necessary mask. It is significant that he is a less personal poet than Smith, though at the same time we can deduce certain things about him. We might for instance deduce that he was a schoolteacher: but his comments are so dry that, though autobiography may be there, it is not the autobiography that remains with us but the creation of a particular world. In other words, future readers will learn from him a great deal of what Edinburgh was like at the time in which he lived and wrote about it.

It does not seem to me that Garioch is ever wholly at home with specifically intellectual material, as for instance in "The Muir." It is true that this poem shows detailed knowledge of relatively recent physics and that the conclusion he draws—that our world as seen in terms of modern science is as ghostly and strange as that which the mad Fergusson saw—is unimpeachable. Nevertheless, this poem lacks the sheer fun of his nature, it is too earnest and he takes science too seriously. The language seems duller and lacks altogether the paradoxes and collisions that animate his best poems.

More satisfying from this point of view is a poem like "Perfect" where he discusses the arts in terms of craftsmanship in wood. It seems to me quite typical that he should have approached the arts from that direction (what a distance it takes him, for instance, from someone like Wallace Stevens) and should have arrived at the funny seriousness of the conclusion that if one is looking for perfection one should turn to the machine. Craftsmanship is very important to him, and it is this above all which sharpens his poems, and not so much the overwhelming light of the imagination. He shares this craftsmanship with other writers of witty poems. And I am quite certain that the sonnet is his form *par excellence*. To this box he assigns his most pungent comments, a box which locks them tightly with a final click and yet which like a jewel case sets them off most sparklingly. His greatest and most daring leaps are not ones of the imagination but are often found in his adventurous and most felicitous rhymes. He must have been fascinated by what is difficult. He has the air of one who sets himself problems, is interested in puzzles, paradoxes, enigmas: he has also the mind of one who is as interested in people as he is in things.

He does not have what might be called a hard streak. It is as if he is speaking from the frailty of his own mortality—"bruckle" is a word he often uses—and is amused and not nauseated by the contradictions and pomposities he sees all around him. Those provosts and other officials belong to a species that is recognisably human and yet, curiously enough, diffused in the light of the imagination they appear like coloured butterflies observed on a fine summer's day. How extraordinarily sunnily they inhabit the world of a Shostakovitch or a Mozart and how even the phrase "thon yin's" is sparklingly airy and compassionate.

One finds it hard not to visualise the author himself when one reads his poems, they are so much a part of him, so truly his voice. They are so exactly by a man who delighted in life, the life that was all around him: a long supple worm emerges out of a pavement to welcome a shower that does not, after all, exist, only to find that it is water with which Garioch is cleaning the stone. In this sense he has much of the affection for animals that Burns had. Of all the Scottish poets of this century, he is the closest in many ways to the ordinary person, risking at times a tenderness which might belong to the kailyard, as when he writes of the "lambies soukan their mammies." Nevertheless, it is only rarely that one finds such a lapse, if lapse it is, for it is difficult to find a Garioch poem of which one can say quite simply, "It is a bad poem."

But he is unlike Burns in that we find in his poetry also a deep darkness which is disquieting and which only his craftsmanship can contain. If he is the clown in one way, he is also the clown in another way in that he is more aware than most of the fragility of things. Time and time again he refers to the frail crust which may be cracked open at any time to reveal a landscape of worms, rats, rotted timbers. He broods much on Fergusson's madness: he creates a picture of pastoral landscape only to hear the pig "scraunch til the wrang gode, Help, Help." If "Brither Worm" reminds us by its ending of Lawrence's "Snake" there is far more of horror in it than in the work of one who welcomed the darkness as light's more creative brother. Suddenly a man who comes into Garioch's house from a Jaguar flashes a "well-dentured fang" and the poet catches a glimpse of near-forgotten hell. He closes his shutters against his father's ghostly face. He sees on a moor "bluid dreipan" down among the roots. He flings away a cigarette end and sees in its place a "bleizan plane" over Africa. He converts military drill into an exercise in hysteria, that guarantee of sanity against unbearable orthodoxy. Ghosts return to haunt the powerful and the ruthless. More than is the case with most modern poets, there is a strain of mediaeval horror at the heart of Garioch's work. It is snatched from the inferno.

Thus it is no longer the observer we see but the man who is as frightened as we are ourselves, who is kept sane by the rigid forms of his verse.

This is a complicated man, a man who can make beautiful rhymes for Antisyzygy but who can also see life as a "bogle-hauntit" dream. According to this poetry, most work of the kind that we do is meaningless, and there is a lovely fitness in the line from "Owre Weill":

Ye're faur owre weill to wark the day.

That is why Garioch appeals to us so much, he is so very like ourselves, for we all at times feel as he does the glory and the horror. We are most of us small people condemned to be on the edge of a parade or a feast which, though perhaps desired, is essentially hollow. We have most of us been at some time or other in the power of the ignorant and petty and bureaucratic. We are all struck by the contradictions that burst around us continually.

It is Garioch's great gift that he was not overwhelmed by the darknesses he saw but by sheer craftsmanship was able to bury them in the box of the sonnet so that later they are resurrected as hilarious and light. Above all it is, I think, in the translations from Belli that we see that extraordinary control which allows so much local anarchy. Who else would have found three rhymes for Spagna, and two for Wamphray? It is in the exuberance of the rhymes that much of the celebratory joy appears: for there, once seen, the unpredictable is made inevitable.

Garioch never attempted the heights of a MacDiarmid (nor did he find security in any ideology): his two feet were planted on a ground that was continually in danger of disappearing. Others may refer to the brilliant way in which he handled Scots, but I think he is an exemplar for anyone who wishes to write in that language in a truly contemporary way and with a truly modern consciousness.

Hugh MacDiarmid's
A Drunk Man Looks at the Thistle

What strikes me about *A Drunk Man Looks at the Thistle* is that it seems to be a turning point in MacDiarmid's work, though at the same time a partial continuation of it (for example in the spatial images). Before it he wrote hallucinatory lyrics, after it we find him engaged in a quest for belief. *A Drunk Man* shows him in an uneasy poise, whether he should push the hallucinatory to its limits or whether in order to survive one must select and categorise. This seems to me to be the main importance of the poem. It can on the whole be explicated clearly enough, and much has been written about it. It shows the see-saw movement of a mind, it is among other things an attack on the bourgeoisie, that is, on categorisation. The bourgeois is a contented but dead man because he has made his selection: he has categorised experience. He is like:

> Staundin water in a pocket o'
> Impervious clay.

He feeds from the "common trough." MacDiarmid, however, says that he himself is more complex than that:

> I'll hae nae hauf-way house, but aye be whaur
> Extremes meet

The thistle represents the tortuous ascent towards the creation of a worthwhile self. The moonlight is that ideal self, perfect and complete.

> For ilka thing a man can be or think or dae
> Aye leaves a million mair unbeen, unthocht, undune,
> Till his puir warped performance is
> To a' that micht ha' been, a thistle to the mune.

It is this which torments him: to select a persona as the bourgeois has done is to omit all other possibilities. The moonlight is ideal freedom, the thistle represents the demands of morality which contorts ideals and development.

The world is swamped in subjectivity: is he himself the thistle or the thistle him? (This kind of thing reminds one of Rilke whom MacDiarmid had at this time read). The thistle is his "ain skeleton." "The munelicht ebbs and flows and wi't my thocht." The thistle is transformed by an extraordinary series of images into bagpipes, alligators, bellows, Mephistopheles in heaven, a skeleton at a tea meeting, the missing link, and so on. It breed roses of perfection. It is also the thistle in a bride's hand instead of roses. The moonlight is heaven and himself offscourings. The thistle is a "knot of nerves." The moonlight is his knowledge of creativity. It reminds him also of the Cross. It is like a horse's skin "aneth a cleg" or the Northern Lights. (It is astonishing how fertile MacDiarmid's imagination is at this stage, so that by using the simplest props, a thistle, a drunk man and moonlight, he can juxtapose them perpetually in new combinations. It is like something Charlie Chaplin might do with a hat, a stick, baggy trousers, and a moustache).

At the same time he wants to be like the thistle:

>   Be like the thistle, O my soul,
>   Heedless o' praise and quick to tak' affront,
>   And growin' like a mockery o' a'
>   Maist life can want or thole,
>   And manifest forevermair
>   Contempt o' ilka goal.
>
>   O' ilka goal—save ane alane;
>   To be yoursel', whatever that may be.
>   And as contemptuous o' that,
>   Kennin' nocht's worth the ha'en, . . .

The thistle in the moonlight is also like a skeleton with a spirit in it, it is epileptic, a brain laid bare, a nervous system. . . . What does all this mean? On the one page MacDiarmid says that the only worthwhile task is to be oneself: on the other hand to be oneself is nothing:

>   And fain I would be free
>   O' my eternal me.

The poem proceeds by a see-saw dialectic. It might be worth saying something about this. The dialectic is not a logical one in a Hegelian or Marxist sense. What I believe is happening is that the dialectic arises from a conflict between art and life. Art demands form, but life is formless. To reconcile the two on the highest level is impossible. Life is continually making art appear minor. Therefore, whenever MacDiarmid makes an artistic statement, he recognises that life can negate it. All human selves are imperfect. The bourgeoisie have made selves but they have done this at the expense of losing life. I do not think that it is the selectiveness of the bourgeoisie that drives MaDiarmid to despair, it is the smugness that accompanies it. It is their lack of recognition that they have in fact made a selection.

I think myself that at this very point MacDiarmid was confronted by a problem which is impossible to solve. For all practical purposes, when we are confronted by a logical or mathematical paradox, we can forget about it: in life we have to live perpetual paradoxes. We cannot dismiss them: we have to endure them.

To select from experience and to set up categories is to limit one's experience. Not to select is to die from a plethora of images. What one sees in this poem is a man creating a clearing in order momentarily to exist. There are manic sets of images crowding in on him and these represent the multifariousness of life perpetually raging around him. The creation of the artistic image and artistic order is a strategy by which for the moment the poet survives.

MacDiarmid cannot be content with bourgeois life precisely because it leaves out all the savagery and glory of life. On the other hand his life as poet depends on being as inclusive as possible. The contorted thistle is a compromise. Women (for instance his wife) prevent him fully from experiencing this inclusive life again, but it is only through women that such a life can be sensed. Women are socially conservative, but on the other hand biologically they can release one into that wider world. Sex is therefore very important in this poem. MacDiarmid wants to be free of the control of women and yet only women can save him as a poet. Woman tethers him:

> Or dost thou mak' a thistle o' me, wumman? But for thee
> I were as happy as the munelicht, withoot care . . .

On the other hand

> . . . ilka evening fey and fremt
> (Is it a dream nae waukenin' proves?)
> As to a trystin'-place undreamt,
> A silken leddy darkly moves.

My own impression of this poem is that it cannot be categorised (or even criticised properly) for the simple reason that its main purpose is to resist categorisation. It is a poem written at a crucial point in MacDiarmid's life. It is not a distanced poem as *The Waste Land* is. He is implicated in an insoluble problem precisely because it is a life problem. To select is to be untrue to experience (and he wants all experience), but on the other hand not to select (and thus experience everything indiscriminately) is to be destroyed. I think it can safely be said that if MacDiarmid had continued on this level his psyche would have been annihilated.

I have seen essays and reviews of this poem but none which states the central dilemma clearly. They pass aesthetic judgments on an existential poem which demands experiencing. The possible solutions to the life problem in the poem might be that either MacDiarmid would cease to write (is this what the ending means?) or that he would select and categorise. I think that by selecting Communism he did the latter, though perhaps not consciously. From the point of view attained in this poem (admittedly an inhumanly difficult one), the bourgeoisie and Communism are both betrayals since they both abstract from a plethora of possible worlds. On the other hand, to have maintained the poise of the poem where every statement breeds its opposite and every argument its counter-argument, would have been impossible, for on the evidence of this poem MacDiarmid had a capacity for feeling the complexities of life to a far more piercing degree than is common even among poets.

It seems to me that to compare this poem with *The Waste Land* may not after all be fruitful except superficially. *The Waste Land* is a distanced artefact. Though it was produced in a moment of crisis in Eliot's life (it is interesting that both poets had to have the help of others to cut their work into manageable proportions) he succeeded by an enormous effort in creating a structure which can stand apart from him more than the *Drunk Man* does for MacDiarmid. *A Drunk Man* is a much rawer poem than *The Waste Land*, much more immediate and vertiginous. The sexual passages, for instance, are much more vitally coarse and less mannered than Eliot's, and where Eliot's colloquialisms sound artificial (he does not really know about the working classes) the democratic structure of Scotland allows MacDiarmid to be colloquial in a more natural way. Thus MacDiarmid can create a ladder from the primitive to the sophisticated without any sense of linguistic strain.

At a certain stage MacDiarmid was willing, or was compelled, to open himself out to life, and being of an extremely sensitive nature he was nearly destroyed. Yet he wished to retain such insights, for he knew that his life as a poet was dependent on them. He was being more extreme that one had the power to be—and survive. But to survive—was that worth it when one could survive only as a bourgeois and lead a living death?

Basically the poem is a confessional one. It has more to do with Sylvia Plath and Robert Lowell than many care to think, and this gives it much of its power. I feel that comparisons which do not recognise this are irrelevant since they are merely applying aesthetic categories to what is existential through and through. MacDiarmid is confronting a question and living an experience which is crucial to his art. On the answer, if he can find it, depends his future. He is staking his consciousness on the outcome. Of course there is no answer, and this accounts for the feeling one has that the poem could go on forever. There is only the swaying movement of a mind which on its journey uncovers an enormous wealth of interesting and brilliant material.

The hallucinatory power of the lyrics is in this poem, too, but it has come into a head-on clash with the world. If the lyrics are the poems of his Innocence then this poem is the poem of Experience. He has come into the Vale of Soul-making.

—from *Studies in Scottish Literature* (1970)

The Golden Lyric:
The Poetry of Hugh MacDiarmid

I

When one discusses the poetry of Hugh MacDiarmid one is forced to make an evaluation of the importance of ideas in poetry or, to put it another way, how ideas are related if at all to poetry. Now it is quite clear that a poem is not simply a system of formal ideas. Poetry is not a putting of an idea into verse. It is not enough to have an idea and then to put that idea into verse forms. The classic case of a poem built up on an idea is the *De Rerum Natura* of Lucretius. Nevertheless, it could be argued that the parts of Lucretius's poem which are the best poetry are those which deal not simply with ideas in the abstract but rather with death faced without hope.

The logic of poetry is not the logic of a Kant or a Hegel. It is not a question of proving anything in the sense that one proves something in geometry, for instance. Nor should one expect from a poet or any artist a purely logical mind (however much an artist may be betrayed into hankering after this).

What ideas as such has a poet ever bequeathed to the human race? Wordsworth was possessed to a certain extent of ideas and made an attempt to create a system of thought in relation to poetry, but Coleridge showed without much difficulty that the basis of his ideas was demonstrably false and removed from reality. It is not the case that country people have purer feelings than city people. It is an education to see how Coleridge demolishes Wordsworth's painfully created structure. For to think is very difficult: to think originally is so difficult that the few who have achieved it can be counted in the hundreds. What poet has shown a power of clear thought? And if he could think clearly, what value would this have for his poetry? If we want logic we should go to a logician. If we want sociology we should go to a sociologist. If we want politics we should go to a politician. That is not the poet's job.

It is a well-known fact that scientists, outside their own chosen field, have opinions which are trivial in essence. Bertrand Russell has a passage where he says that if you were to ask a scientist for his ideas on anything outside his own chosen field his supposed power of thought would collapse, revealing only personal emotive flickers, not dignified enough to justify the name of ideas. In this impotence outside their own work they are like other men. Their power of thought serves them little: and in fact many of them may even be more stupid and removed from reality than common people without their ability. It may be that Russell himself sometimes shows this idealistic stupidity.

Nevertheless, it is true that poets have often felt the need to write about ideas. They are impelled to this by a feeling of helplessness. They feel perhaps that their poetry isn't changing the world, and they had possibly expected in their youth that this might happen. MacDiarmid himself says at one point that if the common people—the masses—do not know his poetry, then he has failed. They feel that art is not accomplishing anything. They look out into the world of action and they feel a certain envy. No one seems to be listening to them. Pure aesthetic creations are not being valued. The Lenins of this world are the important people. And therefore they feel that they must introduce Thought into their work. Surely people will read it if it is permeated with Thought, with Ideas.

This argument, however, seems essentially false. Thought put into poetry does not necessarily make good verse. It is not from Thought alone that poetry begins. And furthermore, if only one idea is being promulgated then the poetry becomes propaganda. Yeats says that a quarrel with oneself makes poetry but that a quarrel with others makes rhetoric. This is true. It is true because the level on which the poet works must not be exclusive. Any thinking person who has thought long and deeply—or even felt long and deeply—must realise that no one dogma is sufficient to interpret for us the meaning of the universe (if it has a meaning). A poet knows this better than anyone else. Another thing that Yeats said was that man can embody truth but not know it. One way of interpreting this might be that a poet could write about a man who believes he has the truth: to claim that he knows the truth about himself would be ludicrous. Now it is true that the movement of MacDiarmid's verse recognises the difficulty of arriving at the truth. In *A Drunk Man Looks at the Thistle* he hopes that he will be preserved from those people who think that they know the truth and are possessed of it. He says that sometimes he bursts out laughing when he remembers how small and trivial he himself is when set up against the scale of the universe. One knows perfectly well what he is talking about. He is talking about the self-satisfied Scotsman whom he ridicules in the *Drunk Man* by pitching him out into the stars to show him how unimportant he really is. One can see why in Scotland above all MacDiarmid might time and time again break himself against this colossal pride and ignorance. And to be fair to him, he writes most often from this stance.

There are times, too, however, when MacDiarmid gives the impression that he himself knows the truth and that his ideas are essentially right. In this perhaps he is being infected by his Scottish environment and the stubborn, blind, unbreakable Scottish will. For the question is this: if people are not convinced by these ideas logically and in prose why should they be convinced when they are put into poetry and their rigour is gone?

However, MacDiarmid's favourite method seems to be a dialectic one. He may have learned this from a study of Communism, but he was talking about Hegel before Communism came into his poetry. In this method he veers about from one idea to its opposite. And very often he comes down on neither side.

An example of this kind of argument occurs in the section of the *Drunk Man* when one verse says:

> I'm no like Burns and weel I ken
> Tho' any wench can ser',
> It's no' through mony but through yin
> That ony man wuns fer. . . .

and a good many verses later:

> He's no a man ava',
> And lacks a proper pride,
> Gin less than a' the warld
> Can ser' him for a bride!

It would be pointless to single out all the instances of this kind of movement in his poetry. It is the most pronounced movement of his verse, the way in which he constructs a poem, especially his poems of ideas. Sometimes this dialectic can become almost ridiculous: for example, from "Second Hymn to Lenin":

> Ah, Lenin, you were richt. But I'm a poet
> (And you cud mak allowances for that!)
> Aimin' at mair than you aimed at
> Tho' yours comes first, I know it.
>
> An unexamined life is no worth ha'in'.
> Yet Burke was richt: owre muckle concern
> Wi' life's foundations is a sure
> Sign o' decay: tho' Joyce in turn
>
> Is richt. . . .

Now clearly the dialectic movement in poetry is not uncommon and can be very exciting. However, if the poem remains *on the level of the idea* no final result can ever be arrived at. And often one feels with MacDiarmid that in fact he does not resolve his poems as poetry. The ideas are built up in a staggering profusion, like an insane stair, and no resolution seems to be possible.

In one of his poems—the famous "The Seamless Garment"—what in fact is achieved by the poem as such? It is true that it is finely conversational. He is explaining to a mill hand, in terms of what the mill hand can understand, what Lenin was like. He says that the weaver is at home with the loom and Lenin was at home with working class life. His knowledge of the working class had become second nature to him. Similarly with Rilke. Rilke too had created a seamless garment. MacDiarmid asks the weaver whether he turns out good or shoddy clothes. He says that the worker would not want to go back to the old days and the old machines. He says that machinery has improved but man has not. He says that the threads lie hundreds to the inch (in the same way as communists to the cell—which is not really a very good simile but probably just as good as some of C. Day Lewis's). The poem ends with MacDiarmid saying that what he wants is integrity too. Now all this is very well but it is really a very tame conclusion for such a poem, painfuly built up. Is this all, then? Is MacDiarmid just ending with a prayer and recognition of his own impotence? The poem has not been resolved in terms of poetry though the ideas move beautifully.

If we turn to another poem to find a typical dialectic movement one would perhaps turn to a poem like "Easter 1916." In this poem Yeats recognises that dedication to an ideal can make a stone of the heart: but at the same time this dedication can make men heroic. Even the refrain is ambiguous. "A terrible beauty is born." Is there really a pun on the word "terrible"? The poem, in spite of its dialectic, does give an impression of attaining a poise which holds within it all the various possibilities inherent in it and in the argument. These men might have been ridiculous: on the other hand they might have been heroic. Great actions may really be brought to birth by fools or clowns. Or was it a great action after all?

All this is true. But the poem does not convince us by its ideas. It convinces by its language, by its pathos and its music, by the feeling that the whole of Yeats is concerned in this poem and not just his mind. One feels that for Yeats this event was a human event. It has not only changed these men: it has changed Yeats. It will possibly change us. But it will not change us simply because of the ideas. It will change Yeats because he is humanly shocked into a state in which these ideas become real for him. They will make a human change in him, not simply a mental one. One feels with MacDiarmid's poem and with much else of his poetry of ideas that in fact he himself is not changed humanly. He has only seen with his mind, not felt with his heart. "O wae's me on this weary wheel."

Now the course of MacDiarmid's progress can be charted fairly clearly. The first two or three books are books of lyrics mainly. Then there is the long poem, *A Drunk Man*, on the whole successful because the dialectic there is freshly felt and at the same time the dialectic suits the drunk man. This is, of course, MacDiarmid to a great extent: in spite of the left-handed tribute that MacDiarmid pays to Scottish education, what Scot would be able to quote T. S. Eliot (among many others) as well as translate from the Russian at this time? Then after that we have *To Circumjack Cencrastus*.

Now this poem begins by using the image of the snake, but it is not long till the snake disappears. In the previous poem the thistle by a series of almost miraculous images, both grave and gay, with pathos and bravado, held the poem together: the snake does not hold its successor together. The poem itself is a ragbag of ideas. It contains a lot about MacDiarmid himself and the beginnings of his hatred of employers. Parts of this poem—especially towards the end—are very bitter and personal. It is clear from this poem onwards that MacDiarmid is going to be more and more concerned with ideas for their own sake. But there is one astonishing brilliance in the poem and that is the really fine translation of Rilke's "Requiem to Paula Modersohn." (MacDiarmid often refers to Rilke in his poetry: and yet in many ways the poets are very different.)

After *To Circumjack Cencrastus* we are well on the way to the kind of poetry we get in *In Memoriam James Joyce*, though here and there in the stony waste we get some marvellous things like "On a Raised Beach," "The Little White Rose," parts of the "Lament for the Great Music," "At my Father's Grave," the savage "At the Cenotaph" and the eerie passage from the poem on Glasgow beginning "Where have I seen a human being looking . . ." and many more.

Having read the whole of MacDiarmid's poetry as far as I was able to I have now come to the conclusion that MacDiarmid did take a wrong turning when he began on his poetry of ideas. At one time I did not believe this because I felt that cleverness and intelligence were very important. I still believe this, but on the other hand I would not give them the high position that I once did. Now I believe there were a number of reasons for MacDiarmid to take this turning. The first reason is that he is naturally a very intelligent man. I do not mean by this that he is a great thinker for clearly this would be wrong, and he would not claim this himself. I believe that a poet by definition cannot be a great thinker. However, he clearly has a restless and inquiring mind. He has also always been a great lover of books, as he mentions in his autobiography. Therefore it was natural that he be led towards ideas and an investigation of them.

Secondly I believe that after the creation of his lyrics MacDiarmid, with that curious distrust that poets have about the value of something simply because of its smallness, felt that he ought to move on to more "serious" work. This I believe to have been a profound error, not the fact that he should have moved on, for perhaps he could not prevent himself from doing this, but the fact that he should think a poetry of ideas must necessarily be a more "serious" poetry. I believe that "The Watergaw" is in every way far more serious than anything he produced on the basis of ideas alone. These long poems may be intellectually exciting, but they are not serious. They do not confront us with serious things. They do not, I think, react on us as whole human beings. Their explorations are not deep enough. This may seem a very odd thing to say when the present writer admits that there are great stretches of them that he cannot understand. Nevertheless, MacDiarmid was making the assumption that by injecting ideas into his work he would become serious. What poems could be more serious than Blake's lyrics (a poet I shall return to later), and yet are they full of ideas in any detachable sense?

A mention of Hegel, a reference to Einstein, an allusion to a book here and there, does not make a poem serious. In fact MacDiarmid here is showing a snobbery, a kind of aristocracy.

A third reason, I think, was that he was running out of Scottish material. After all MacDiarmid undoubtedly has genius. To be born in Scotland and to be a genius might seem an ironical joke. What is there in Scotland for a poet after a while? Very few human beings of consequence. A blankness without a public. And rather than write poems about Glencoe, etc., etc. MacDiarmid was driven towards a poetry of ideas since no human poetry was possible to him at that stage. Let it not be thought that the present writer is passing judgment on MacDiarmid at this point. His reasons and compulsions for what he did appear almost inevitable, but not perhaps with the inevitability of the poetic impulse. Again I think he must have been influenced by Burns and the disastrous post-Burns era. The kind of poetry written then had little or no intellectual content. Very well, then, MacDiarmid must have thought, let us inject intellectual content into it. It is true that Burns's poetry had little intellectual content. However, it has human content. It is not because of lack of intellectual content that Burns's poetry often fails but rather because the human content is falsified. "Holy Willie's Prayer" is a great poem because it is exactly observed. "The Cotter's Saturday Night" is poor because the human content is false. In the latter poem Burns was not telling the truth. Intellectual content would not have saved it.

Finally, MacDiarmid must have been influenced by poems like *The Waste Land* and the wanderings of Ezra Pound. MacDiarmid often refers admiringly to Eliot in his work ("Eliot, a good Scots name," he says at one point) and elsewhere he remarks that *A Drunk Man* is a better poem than *The Waste Land*. One does not want to venture into comparisons now: to distinguish which is better would be very difficult. Rather, however, one can notice in MacDiarmid's poetry the same tricks as in Eliot and Pound, the references to abstruse facts, the in-group authors, the quotations fitted into the text, and counterpointing. This seems to work in *A Drunk Man* but in later poetry the stretches become more and more arid, "a moment of joy is harder to get." Perhaps they come closer really to the Cantos of Pound which are practically incomprehensible.

To put the point as bluntly as possible, I would give away whole swaths of MacDiarmid's later work for "The Watergaw" alone, which seems to me to be a poem about human beings at a human crisis however it was conceived, whereas practically everything in his later books can be got equally well from their sources if one wants to read them.

II

It may be strange to say this, but when I read MacDiarmid's poetry at length I often think of that essay which Eliot wrote on Blake. One might wonder what Blake had to do with MacDiarmid or what the point of the comparison is. Now in this essay Eliot maintained that Blake had been led astray by a hotch-potch of ideas which are completely uninteresting in themselves. It might be useful for someone to take this comparison between Blake and MacDiarmid further (the present writer doesn't have the detailed knowledge for it).

It is sufficient to say that here are two poets—Blake and MacDiarmid—who both begin with lyrics of a certain kind, that is, lyrics which contain a fusion of the intellect and the feeling which is highly unusual and at times hallucinatory. Both poets go on to write long poems based rather insecurely on systems which are fairly private (even MacDiarmid's Communism doesn't seem to be all that orthodox). Both have little to do with the classical tradition (it is interesting that MacDiarmid very seldom refers to the Greeks and Trojans from whom so many poems have been quarried but rather goes back to Celtic sources). Blake too does not seem interested in a classical tradition but goes back to sources found nearer home. Both are radical in their views though they have the basic aristocratic attitude of poets. They write about freedom and the spirit of the man in chains.

Another similarity which I wish to stress for a particular reason is that neither had a university training. Now let no one under any circumstances believe that I consider a university training obligatory or even important for a poet. Nothing could be further from the truth. On the other hand I often feel that in comparison with the mind of Eliot the mind of MacDiarmid is untrained, and sometimes it seems to me irresponsible. Eliot's critical work is far superior to MacDiarmid's such as it is. No, what I am saying is this: I cannot see any justification for MacDiarmid's writing much of his later work in verse form. Eliot too had certain things he felt like saying but he developed a prose style for them. I am not saying that all of Eliot's work or indeed much of Eliot's work outside his purely literary criticism is of much value, but at least he made the distinction between the things he could say in prose and the things he could say in poetry. I feel that MacDiarmid might have done better to make the same distinction.

If this comparison with Blake be accepted on a certain level it will be seen that there is a certain progress in the work of each of them.

Now MacDiarmid became a Communist of a particular kind at a particular stage in his career. It may be for all I know that there are signs of Communist thinking at the end of *To Circumjack Cencrastus* when he attacks his boss on a personal level, and he may well have been forced into it by his later personal sufferings (and here may one say how much one admires the kind of personal integrity that MacDiarmid has shown?) and also by what he saw around him in the 1930s especially. He wasn't the only one to be attracted by such a system then though I don't think that MacDiarmid could be systematised for long.

However, I do not think that MacDiarmid is a Communist in any ordinary sense of the word. True, he writes in approval of certain of Lenin's actions and in these poems a certain inhumanity emerges. But that MacDiarmid has much in common with the masses I do not believe. How can one prove this, that MacDiarmid is not a Communist? There is only one test. When is his poetry at its best, at its most complex in a good way? MacDiarmid may think he is a Communist but I think on the other hand that his imagination betrays him.

I would suggest that excluding his early work up to the *Drunk Man*, the burden of MacDiarmid's imagination does not emerge in his Communist poems nor on the whole do they convince me imaginatively in any way. For after all the poems about Lenin are about the integrity which will allow MacDiarmid to make good poetry than they are about politics. I would suggest that the burden of MacDiarmid's imagination in his later work can be found where he writes about exclusiveness and not where he writes about involvement with humanity. I am thinking in particular about "On a Raised Beach" which seems to me his finest achievement after *A Drunk Man*, a poem about stones and an appalling apartness. It is in this kind of conscious loneliness that MacDiarmid is most imaginatively convincing. It could indeed be argued that the progress of MacDiarmid is from the human to a poetry of landscape and stones and language. It is the aristocratic lonely voice in these poems that convinces. (In fact he seems to me to become astonishingly like Yeats in thought if not in style.) The poems about the masses do not really have much resonance.

If Communism among other things means a concern with people, then MacDiarmid is not a Communist. If Communism among other things means the patience of a Lenin—the patience of stones—then there are these things in the poems. But on the other hand they are there—the ruthlessness and the violence—academically, as in Lewis Grassic Gibbon. It is not easy to know how MacDiarmid would have reacted to the turmoil of a real Communist revolution in his own country and to the possible murders and killings. I myself find much of what he says about Lenin distasteful. (This problem of violence is to be found in Grassic Gibbon and, in our own time, in the poetry of Gunn and MacBeth, for instance.) It is fair enough to say that Lenin had to have a lot of people killed but I do not think that a poet should speak about this without agony for he should try to see people not as faceless masses but as individuals. One should try to imagine what that violence would mean in the last analysis to oneself. That is why I find MacDiarmid's poems about violence somewhat unreal and rhetorical. The poems of those who have suffered violence are not like this. (Another thought which might enter one's mind is this: if Scotland had had its Easter Rising, how would this have affected MacDiarmid's poetry? Yeats saw war close to him and at times was horrified).

In the later MacDiarmid there is really a great loneliness and coldness. I think his poetry about stones is often magnificent and proud, and it convinces me that it is poetry and not propaganda. It is not a question of approving or disapproving of this poetry. The poetry convinces one whether one likes it or not. That is why I often remember a snatch of dialogue between two characters in one of Faulkner's novels. One of them is praising "Ode to a Nightingale." The other simply remarks that Keats had to write something, didn't he? And I feel this with the later MacDiarmid, that in his latest work he had to write something and he wrote about Communism and various other ideas. That is not at all a question of saying that MacDiarmid was insincere. It is more profound than that. A man may say that he is a Communist and in the recesses of his imagination not be so. Milton was of the devil's party without knowing it. MacDiarmid's later poetry convinces me when he is at his most aristocratic, a cold eagle, a man in love with stones. This part of him—the truest part of him at this stage—knows that he is not like other people, that they have very little to say to him, that he cannot learn anything from them and that they'll never learn anything anyway.

Again it is not a question of my approving or disapproving of this—and I can see quite clearly how he might have arrived at this position, in Scotland—it is merely to say what kind of poetry seems to me to be successful. Whether for instance Eliot says he is Anglo-Catholic, Royalist and classical seems to me to be irrelevant. It has little to do with his most successful poetry, or even with his truest preoccupations in poetry.

III

If I were therefore to pick MacDiarmid's best books I would pick his earlier ones right up to the *Drunk Man*.

The latter I think is a major work on many levels though MacDiarmid finds difficulty with the ending. I am not sure that I completely understand the section about silence, though in his introduction David Daiches seems quite sure that he understands it. But on balance the image of the thistle and the moonlight does in fact hold the poem together and holds it at the same time in a real world. The later poems seem to me not to be able to get hold of a symbol which will be a unifying thread. Here too in this poem a lot of what he says later is said for the first time and said freshly. I often wonder whether in fact some of *To Circumjack Cencrastus* may not consist of passages rejected from the previous poem.

In a sense the dialectic seems to work for this poem partly because the symbolism helps it to. The basic groundwork of the poem, which in effect is the struggle towards consciousness of a man and of a nation and of humanity, is represented lucidly by the thistle and the moonlight. The thistle can be seen to stand for the man distorted by morality and the pressures of existence. The moonlight can be seen to stand for the Platonic idea, unflawed, complete and deadly.

The fact too that the thistle is the Scottish emblem allows MacDiarmid to pass from the personal to the national very easily. It is clear also that to a certain extent he does allow the main character to be different from himself. The protagonist is not wholly himself, though he does have a great deal of the various knowledge of MacDiarmid. He seems to represent something essentially Scottish. He goes back to Tam o' Shanter, one supposes, and is a human being in whose twists and turns we are interested.

The change in mood and thought (which in others of the poems may seem arbitrary) does not seem so in this poem because after all the protagonist is a drunk man. It is a very witty poem, the poem of a writer who has not allowed himself to be overwhelmed by the world. One senses in *To Circumjack Cencrastus* a kind of bitterness of which there is little sign in the *Drunk Man*. MacDiarmid in this poem is still able to objectify his insights without rancour. He can be playful in a very funny way as, for instance, in the passage about the Chinese at the Burns supper.

The poem does not seem to me to reach any conclusion but it does not seem to matter very much for it is redeemed by so many other qualities, wit, humour, snatches of strange balladic verses, and in general a healthy tone.

Nevertheless, in spite of all this, and in spite of the fact that in variety, interest in humanity, glitterings of wit, and sustained rhetoric, this poem must undoubtedly be considered major, and in spite of the brilliant use to which MacDiarmid puts his symbolism—externalising and internalising the thistle from one moment to another and doing the same with the moonlight (it is perhaps this he learnt from Rilke if he learnt anything)—in spite of the fact that there is a great richness in the poem, one still comes back to the earliest poems of all, and one or two lyrics here and there among the later poems.

Essentially MacDiarmid is at his greatest in his lyric poems. Even the *Drunk Man* itself is a collection of lyrics to a great extent and this is proved by the manner in which MacDiarmid himself has presented the poem in his *Collected Poems* (1962), by detached sections. In general he hasn't quite the architectural power necessary for the true long poem and it may be that this is no longer possible anyway.

It is a part of my argument therefore to say that in many of these long poems what he is in effect doing is setting up arguments and then knocking them down with others. Also they lack (these later ones) that which we look for in the greatest poetry, insights into human beings. I believe that it is in the early poems that MacDiarmid is concerned with people and their feelings and that later this disappears even when paradoxically he is claiming to be a Communist. But this is not the whole of my argument. I believe it goes deeper than this.

I believe that what happened to MacDiarmid is as follows. He began as the poet with both a masculine and feminine sensibility and eventually allowed the masculine elements in his nature to dominate his work, therefore becoming to a great extent less human than he once was.

For what we find in the early MacDiarmid and miss later is a real tenderness, a real feminine love. It may be strange to say this about MacDiarmid whom one thinks of above all as masculine and a fighter. But I believe that he surrendered or lost a priceless thing when this disappeared from his poetry except now and again. It is for this tenderness, and for a kind of hallucinatory quality which owes little to logic or reason that I above all value MacDiarmid.

I should like to say at this point before proceeding that this idea is not new, this idea of the poet being both masculine and feminine at his best. Coleridge remarked on it when writing about Shakespeare. In our own day Robert Graves talks about it. And I believe that it is this insight gained by using both sides of his nature that makes the greatest of all poets. I would maintain that on the basis of the lyrics alone MacDiarmid must be placed very high indeed, and I think that in the last analysis when the judgment of literary history has been made that it will be on this side that the scales will come down.

It might also at this point be worth mentioning the distinction Coleridge makes between the Fancy and the Imagination, when one attempts an interpretation of MacDiarmid's lyrics. Some of the lyrics are fanciful in the Coleridge sense. Another way of explaining the distinction might be by an analysis of various types of jokes. Everyone knows the kind of joke which has been built up from a single point, very often foliated in order to disguise its point of origin. Most jokes are like this, inexorably labouring to a destination through the usual three stages. However, the jokes of the Goons, for instance, or the Marx Brothers reveal a new dimension to reality and in this sense are truly imaginative. They seem to take a leap into a new area beyond ordinary experience. The joke itself can be brief and unfoliated but nevertheless its implications with regard to reality are immense.

I would say that an example of the fanciful lyric is the one called "The Diseased Salmon":

> I'm gled it's no my face,
> But a fozie saumon turnin'
> Deid-white i' the blae bracks o' the pool,
> Hoverin' a wee and syne tint again i' the churnin'.
>
> Mony's the face'll turn
> Like the fozie saumon I see;
> But I hope that mine'll never be ane
> And I can think o' naebody else's I'd like to be.

Here as in the inferior joke the whole point depends on the resemblance between the colour of the salmon and the death colour of a man's face. The rest of the poem is merely foliage around this. A poem which seems to me to be on the border between the fanciful and the imaginative is the one called "Wild Roses":

> Wi' sae mony wild roses
> Dancin' and daffin',
> It looks as tho' a'
> the countryside's laffin'.
>
> But I maun ca' canny
> Gin I'm no' to cumber
> Sic a lichtsome warld
> Wi' my hert's auld lumber.
>
> Hoo I mind noo your face
> When I spiered for a kiss
> 'Ud gae joukin' a' the airts
> And colourin' like this!

This poem is more complex than the previous one and the movement of the verse seems to suggest a greater complexity. But this is fanciful in that the thought can be expressed in intellectual terms and the connections have a logic not far removed from that of the mind. But again this is not wholly true and that is why I said that it is on the border of the imaginative. When, however, we come to "The Watergaw" we see that we are on a different level altogether.

> Ae weet forenicht i' the yow-trummle
> I saw yon antrin thing
> A watergaw wi' its chitterin' licht
> Ayont the on-ding;
> An' I thocht o' the last wild look ye gied
> Afore ye deed!
>
> There was nae reek i' the laverock's hoose
> That nicht—an' nane i' mine;
> But I hae thocht o' that foolish licht
> Ever sin' syne;
> An' I think that mebbe at last I ken
> What your look meant then.

Here the whole poem is a continuous trembling analogous to the trembling on the verge of a revelation. All parts of the poem work to one end. The poem vibrates like the rainbow. The phrase "yow-trummle" anticipates without actually revealing the rest of the poem.

The second section of the first verse comes as an actual surprise so that one has to return to the beginning again. However, no matter how often one goes over this poem one cannot understand by the reason alone how it was created or how the leap from the rainbow to the dying face was made. A kind of shock is achieved which goes beyond logic. MacDiarmid is pointing to something which he himself doesn't understand and we don't either, though at the same time we feel that the image is true and remarkable and is indicating something serious and important. It might be worth examining that single word "wild" which MacDiarmid uses in the first verse. It seems that no other word would quite do it and yet it is not intellectually clear why this should be. One supposes it to mean "distracted," in the sense that with the rain falling in front of it it is distracted from itself as someone's mind is often distracted by the downpours of life. But there is more to it than that. There is a kind of hint of the helplessness of the animal in that use of the word "wild." It is as if the being were a kind of animal dying and unable to communicate with the human being looking at it and the rain itself becomes the barrier to communication as if one were looking at the animal through the bars of a cage. And one might study the use of the word "foolish." Is MacDiarmid saying that there is no meaning to existence? Certainly it would be worth comparing it with other poems about the rainbow. One might, for instance, compare it with the closing lines of Lowell's "The Quaker Graveyard in Nantucket" where one reads of God surviving the rainbow of his will. Again, the strictly fanciful poem by Thomas Campbell on the same subject might show us by contrast the imaginative power of MacDiarmid's lyric.

The point is that the poem defeats the mind and yet the whole being is satisfied by it. There does seem to be a connection between the face dying and the rainbow beyond the rain. (Does the rain represent the tears of the person looking at the dying face?) The connection does not seem to be a religious one, though the rainbow of course has religious connotations. There was Noah's flood and the rainbow.

Whatever the imagination is, there is no doubt that it is what we require in poetry at the highest level. How it operates is incomprehensible. What it creates is strictly speaking incapable of being managed by the mind. This is true on a very slightly lesser level of "The Bonnie Broukit Bairn."

In this poem there are combined in a short space many of the elements which make MacDiarmid's poems distinctive—the concern with the universe and images of it, the intellectual wit, the class distinction, if one cares to call it that (the Cinderella theme in the poem). For the child is contrasted with the women in their beautiful dresses. (We might notice the hissing sound of the first two lines which might be there to reproduce the whispering and the gossip). Then again MacDiarmid may be thinking that Earth is the only planet not named after a god. The daring end is exactly right with the Scottish word "clanjamfrie," which the aristocratic speakers might not know. Others of these lyrics which are roughly on this level are "In the Hedge-back," "The Eemis Stane," "O Wha's the Bride?" (from *A Drunk Man*) and above all "Empty Vessel." "Trompe L'Oeil" is an example of the purely fanciful.

Along with "The Watergaw," the "Empty Vessel" seems to be on the highest level of the imagination. One points to the use of the word "swing"—a word which one associates with children—but the mind is again defeated by this most moving poem. I have already said that in these poems there is a tenderness which the later MacDiarmid seems later to have lost, surrendering himself to the masculine principle of reason. All these poems which I have mentioned illustrate this tenderness in some degree or another, this concern with humanity in an almost feminine way. In another of his poems MacDiarmid remarks how women will look after sick children when people like himself leave them because they are bored. He tells of the patience of women in situations like this. There is a kind of patient looking behind these lyrics, emerging later in a hallucinatory light and revealing what one can only call love. These lyrics are imaginatively in love with the universe. Whatever achievements MacDiarmid made later, nothing comes near to the authority of these lyrics, an authority which rests only on themselves. They demand no proof and ask no questions, or if they do they do not expect an answer. The poems themselves are answers on the imaginative level. The poems answer by music and language and the answer is love, the love which comes from tenderness and care. I know for instance of no poem like "The Bonnie Broukit Bairn." Here there is applied to the universe a parochial language, which seems to make it familiar and loved.

Poets of course will always undervalue poems like these because they are small, but they are making a great mistake. The only authority poetry ultimately has is the imagination. If we cannot claim this power and see it now and again in action how can we defend ourselves against science? When the ideas in the poem are detachable they can be contradicted and often are. MacDiarmid can be contradicted when one discusses his *In Memoriam James Joyce*. He cannot be attacked at all on the level of these lyrics. They are the real proof of his genius. Their loss would be irreparable. The loss of much else of his work would not be.

The lyrics cannot be duplicated elsewhere in literature. In no other lyrics do I find their special combination of imaginative power, tenderness, wit, intelligence (but an intelligence which has not been divorced from the feelings). Clearly it would be difficult to sustain this achievement. However, though it was clear that it was necessary for MacDiarmid to move on, this does not prevent us saying that his lyrics are his greatest achievement. I can imagine most of his other work as being in a certain sense unnecessary, that is poetically unnecessary. The lyrics made themselves necessary. They appeared through him. The will cannot make poetry. Neither can intelligence. That is why poetry is so unfair. But then that is why also it is different from a craft.

—Akros Publications (1967)

The Complete Poems of Hugh MacDiarmid

Here we have MacDiarmid's *Complete Poems* (1978), printed in chronological order and comprising over 1,400 pages.

It is an awesome testimony to the life work of a quite extraordinarily gifted and prolific mind, and a mind that was at its deepest core essentially poetic, that is, continually able to astonish by its capacity for seeing startling resemblances in reality, as for instance a dying face in a rainbow behind rain, or in a currant bush with its exhausted berries a girl that died in childbirth. MacDiarmid had to a far greater extent than is common the image-making faculty so that even in poems otherwise not brilliant there is nearly always a gift, thrown absentmindedly away from the plenitude of his mind.

We begin with the quite ordinary English poems, then enter the tendar world of the lyrics (so redolent of a domestic Scotland, but interpenetrated by immense distances and winds of space) and are then confronted by the undoubted masterpiece of the *Drunk Man* where MacDiarmid improvises brilliant variations on the thistle and the drunk man and the moon, switching from polemic to eerie ballad to intellectual pyrotechnics in the most bewildering and creative way.

These still seem to me to be his highest achievements, though from his explorations of language and creative collisions of facts a new kind of poetry emerges which I think will require analysis in greater depth than I can give here. It is sufficient to say that even in this new poetry the image-making faculty remains though it operates in a less passionate way.

What is above all clear throughout these two volumes is that the same voice of the same man is heard, wayward, argumentative, contradictory, at times spellbindingly eerie and exact, at times (though he would hate this) almost schoolmasterish in the desperate effort to inform, at all times passionate with that intensity that he and Yeats, as he says, have in common, though the English lack it.

Always there is the superb confidence in himself, the unshakeable self-confidence of the great poet, trying to flog a nation into consciousness, ashamed, contemptuous (both of himself and it), a remorseless lover.

For that was what he was of Scotland: time and time again he returns to it as a schoolmaster returns to a pupil, willing it forward into the world of the mind, imagining a day when Scots will be more interested in great art than in football: and above all returning to Glasgow as that infested warren which always stands before him as a warning and a test.

And continually interested in words, and in language itself as a treasury of consciousness and a mode of advancing it. For above all what we have here is a poet who has gone quite beyond "the black rainbows over the Minch"—the history of Scotland in which so many of us are immersed as in a bog—and who can really see Scotland as in true scale to the Infinite.

Forever he is concerned with life and life more abundant, an increase in consciousness; language and poetry used as weapons in opening doors and windows and the very stones themselves. Thus a poem for MacDiarmid is an organic growth, a natural form.

When one considers how few Scottish writers have been able to operate at this level, with such a fecundity of intellect, and yet in his best moments with such a human tenderness, one can only be grateful for the riches of this book.

For in the end, and in spite of everything, MacDiarmid is optimistic because his scale is so vast. His poetry is almost an evolutionary attempt to move the species forward. The risks he took were breathtaking and I think the reason for this is that he was more interested in content than in style. Unlike Pound or Eliot, he hardly even has a style. The "thought" of these writers seems much more parochial and less visionary than his.

He is a very masculine poet, aggressive, harsh and thistly, but justifiably so in his demolition of Roy Campbell in "The Battle Continues," and in his attacks on those lesser people when he sees them standing in the way of the light. Much of the worst of what he wrote would have been unnecessary if he had not felt that he had to educate as well as compose poetry. But all that is part of life and MacDiarmid, though often literary, always gives us the smell of life. Scotland as he wrote had too much of logic already.

As with all great poets what one wants to do is quote and quote as, for instance, "Babes feeding a lion with spoon-meat" or "To see or hear a clock in Glasgow's horrible, like seeing a dead man's watch, still going though he's dead.": and to say of him as he himself writes, "I touched something—and it was alive."

In the end, though, no political system can contain him in the same way as life is uncontainable. Beyond all the encyclopaedias, dictionaries, polemics, eccentricities of the educator, outrageous statements, MacDiarmid had the gift of the true poet, which is to startle and sometimes amaze in an almost hallucinatory manner.

These two volumes of MacDiarmid's *Complete Poems* are a priceless heritage.

—from *The Glasgow Herald* (7 December 1978)

MacDiarmid and Ideas
with special reference to "On a Raised Beach"

I must say that I have always had difficulty with MacDiarmid's longer poems, more so than with his lyrics, and it seems to me that his poetry of "fact" requires some form of criticism such as we haven't yet got. These longer poems—such as "On a Raised Beach"—I find puzzling mainly because I think they require not my poetic assent but my intellectual assent. "On a Raised Beach" is about stones, but so too is "The Eemis Stane." However, when we read the latter poem we are not required to give intellectual assent, we are rather presented with an image which the poet leaves with us to make what we wish of it. A poem like "On a Raised Beach" is a more difficult structure to deal with. Here and there one finds flashes of imaginative power, of the same intensity as "The Eemis Stane," but the content of the poem as a whole is statement and argument. The problem is that by limiting so much of the poem to statement the poet is allowing the reader to disagree with him at any point along the route. In *The Waste Land* the poet T. S. Eliot does use stone imagery but not in this way. There the imagery is allowed to make its impact imaginatively as simply a notation for barrenness. In "On a Raised Beach" MacDiarmid goes much further than this. The stone is seen as itself and as notation, and it is in the fluctuations between the two ideas that the trouble lies. Thus I can see the stones as MacDiarmid sees them, as the ultimate inhuman audience, that which is obdurate and unchanging, a criterion of loneliness. On the other hand I am troubled by an animism in the poem which seems to me quite close to the poeticisms of someone like Teilhard de Chardin, as if MacDiarmid were investing the stones with thoughts and knowledge of their own. Thus he writes:

> It makes no difference to them whether they are high or low,
> Mountain peak or ocean floor, palace or pigsty.

where he is in fact talking in an animistic way about the "democratic" character of the stones. Again what sense does the following statement make?

> But it is as difficult to understand and have patience here
> As to know that the sublime
> Is theirs, no less than ours. . . .

"I lift a stone," writes MacDiarmid. "It is the meaning of life that I clasp." (But we think of asking, is it any more the meaning of life than lifting a primrose by a river's brim would be?)

I am not saying that any of these statements are untrue: all I am saying is that they allow the reader to think the opposite if he so wishes. It is possible for the reader to say, MacDiarmid is making too much of this. Stones are after all nothing but stones, they have nothing to do with the sublime. There is a difference, for example, between this technique and the way in which stones are used in the verse in Yeats's poem, "Easter 1916":

> Hearts with one purpose alone
> Through summer and winter seem
> Enchanted to a stone
> To trouble the living stream.

There is no question but that there is a sort of nobility in "On a Raised Beach" and that the visionary greatness of the mind that created the poem is of overwhelming brilliance and pathos. But in a strange sense one wonders whether this vision is truly and utterly poetic. It seems in fact to be trying to impose on us in an unpoetic way, as if the poem were an odd sort of propaganda . It is interesting to note how much the poem depends on direct, unambiguous sayings almost like proverbs, as for example:

> The widest open door is the least liable to intrusion

or

> The inward gates of a bird are always open

or

> Impatience is a poor qualification for immortality

or

> Hot blood is of no use in dealing with eternity

These statements sound important, but what in fact do they mean? What does it mean to say "Impatience is a poor qualification for immortality"?

Other statements seem unambiguously correct and undebatable, as for instance:

> What happens to us
> Is irrelevant to the world's geology
> But what happens to the world's geology
> Is not irrelevant to us.

(And yet after thinking about it I am not sure that that statement itself is wholly true).

On the other hand, even if we were to accept the statement as being true, would it lead inevitably to the one that follows it:

> We must reconcile ourselves to the stones
> Not the stones to us.

and what meaning can we apply to such a statement?

'I am not saying that in places the quality of the poetry is not high, but rather that the poet by concentrating so much on statement is allowing too much possibility of contradiction to the reader. Great poetry cannot be contradicted since it doesn't proceed on the level of the idea.

The puzzle about this poem is that on the whole it leaves in the mind a sense of power and illumination and yet in detail it can be argued with. For instance, there is a statement:

> Deep conviction or preference can seldom
> Find direct terms in which to express itself.

He says this because he wishes to show this "deep conviction" as imagined in the stones. But if on the other hand someone were to argue that deep conviction can sometimes appear as volubility, what would this do to the value of the image he has chosen to illustrate the statement? And when he goes on to say:

> I look at these stones and know little about them,
> But I know their gates are open too,
> Always open, far longer open, than any bird's can be. . . .

is he not more or less in the same world as Teilhard de Chardin, that is, seeing the universe in a way which is concerned more with poeticism than with poetry?

Later he says that it is easy to find a "spontaneity here" but that "it is wrong to indulge in these illustrations instead of just accepting the stones."

But why wrong? Is it because such illustrations do not fit his case? And is that therefore what he is doing, that is, making a case? In another part of the poem he says,

> But the world cannot dispense with stones.
> They alone are not redundant. Nothing can replace them
> Except a new creation of God.

For that matter, does he or does he not believe in God?

In what sense is it true to say that the stones are not redundant? In what sense is it truer to say this than to say that air is not redundant or water? In what sense also should one accept the statement:

> Let men find the faith that builds mountains
> Before they seek the faith that moves them.

And he follows this with:

> . . . Men cannot hope
> To survive the fall of the mountains
> Which they will no more see than they saw their rise
> Unless they are more concentrated and determined. . . .

In what sense, one wonders, would one's concentration be enough to allow one to survive the fall of the mountains? And what again does the following statement mean: "These stones go through Man, straight to God, if there is one." (And what, we feel like asking, if there isn't one?)

What have I been trying to say so far? I think I have been trying to say that the "poetry of facts" is not a poetry of facts at all, it is a poetry of ideas with an intention aimed at us: in other words, a poetry of propaganda and persuasion. Such a poetry allows the mind to construct opposites for what is being said. Intelligence is not the real source of poetry nor is, I think, ideas. In a sense, between the passages of poetry the statements are used as connecting links, and the strength of the poem as a whole must depend on our assent to the connecting links.

This poetry is different from the extended verse of Blake's which is vaguer, less dependent on the muscularity of ideas, and is unreadable because of the private symbolism. It is not like the poetry of Milton either, for very often Milton embodies different ideas in different protagonists, and there is no question of Milton saying, "To God, if there is one," with that kind of carelessness.

The strange thing about this poem is that though one may disagree with the ideas, the statements, the links, one finds in places a startling brilliance which convinces not so much by the ideas but rather by a visionary illumination at the point where the stones are seen as themselves, nakedly confronting the poet. I find this, for instance, in the passage beginning:

> Cold, undistracted, eternal, and sublime.
> They will stem the torrents of vicissitude for ever
> With a more than Roman peace.
> Death is a physical horror to me no more.
> I am prepared with everything else to share
> Sunshine and darkness and wind and rain. . . .

and later still, when MacDiarmid is talking of the artist, he writes:

> By what immense exercise of will,
> Inconceivable discipline, courage and endurance,
> Self-purification and anti-humanity,
> Be ourselves without interruption,
> Adamantine and inexorable?

There are, for instance, passages of intense beauty and power but they seem to occur when the intellectual statements fall away and the poet sees the stones naked in front of him and yet at the time shining with the distance that is really between them and him. At those moments the poet is not being animistic. The stones are distant, inhuman, and therefore they become a true image for the inhumanity that he feels he needs. This is not the wheelbarrow of Carlos Williams gleaming in the rain: this is the true inhuman object staring back at that which wishes to be the same. At times like these the poem becomes a great one, when sentences like "Truth has no trouble in knowing itself" fade away and the poet is face to face with the reality and difference of the stones. It is in this stoicism, in this lesson learned from stones—"the rocks rattling in the bead-proof seas"—that we find MacDiarmid at his greatest. The conversation and ideas fall away. It is true that MacDiarmid says that he is not searching for an escape from life and he goes on to explain why this should be so, since the inhumanity of the stones should not represent such a separation. But that is precisely where the weakness of the poem lies, in the explanations, as well as in the strange statements such as the following:

> —I lift a stone; it is the meaning of life that I clasp
> Which is death, for that is the meaning of death;

What my argument comes down to is this: if a poet has to use ideas in poetry let his ideas be as rigorous as those of any other person using ideas, e.g. the philosopher. I do not think the poet has any right to be unrigorous simply because he is a poet. This would apply as much to Lucretius as to MacDiarmid. I do not see that we should apply different criteria to poets as far as ideas are concerned. MacDiarmid was in a different position from Dante for whom there was already a system of ideas in existence. It therefore does make a difference within a system of ideas whether a poet does or does not believe in God, and it is not enough to say casually "whether He exists or not."

As far as this poem is concerned the most powerful image that emerges from it is the confrontation of MacDiarmid with the stones, and the lessons he learns from this confrontation. Many of the other statements are open to contradiction, but his confrontation with them as a human being is not. In this confrontation we are faced with the business of the poet which does not in the end depend on his ideas but rather on this imaginative power to create a convincing situation. And finally the pathos of the poem lies in the change that takes place in the poet, for we sense that by this confrontation he has found the strength, as he says himself, no longer to be afraid of death. What convinces us is the quality of his poetry at the point where this happens, and not the statements of the ideas as such. And in much the same way we are convinced by the change that occurred in Yeats at the point where he was writing "Easter 1916." It is not in other words the stones that matter but the human being looking at the stones. No matter how much the stones are characterised, what technical terms are used, the centre of the poem is MacDiarmid himself: and this is as it should be.

—from P. H. Scott *and* A. C. Davis (eds.),
The Age of MacDiarmid (1980)

Select Bibliography

George Bruce, *Collected Poems* (Edinburgh University Press, 1970)

Stewart Conn, *Thunder in the Air* (Akros, 1967)
The Chinese Tower (Macdonald, 1967)
Stoats in the Sunlight (Hutchinson, 1968)
An Ear to the Ground (Hutchinson, 1972)
Under the Ice (Hutchinson, 1978)

Robert Garioch, *Complete Poetical Works* (Macdonald, 1983)

George Campbell Hay, *Fuaran Sléibh* (William MacLellan, 1947)
O na Ceithir Airdean (Oliver and Boyd, 1952)
Four Points of a Saltire (Reprographia, 1970)
Nua-Bhàrdachd Ghàidhlig (Southside, 1976)

Donald MacAulay, *Seobhrach ás a' Chlaich* (Gairm, 1967)
Nua-Bhàrdachd Ghàidhlig (Southside, 1976)
Oighreachd agus Gabhaltas (Gairm, 1981)

Hugh MacDiarmid, *The Complete Poems of Hugh MacDiarmid* (Martin Brian & O'Keeffe, 1978; Penguin Books, 1985)

Sorley MacLean, *Spring Tide and Neap Tide: Selected Poems 1932-1972* (Canongate, 1977)

Derick Thomson, *Creachadh na Clàrsaich: Plundering the Harp, Collected Poems 1940-1980* (Macdonald, 1982)